# Learning Sales Development with Apex

### Write, Run and Deploy Apex Code with Ease

**Paul Battisson**

www.bpbonline.com

**FIRST EDITION 2020**

**Copyright © BPB Publications, India**

**ISBN: 978-93-89898-18-7**

## Distributors:

**BPB PUBLICATIONS**
20, Ansari Road, Darya Ganj
New Delhi-110002
Ph: 23254990/23254991

**DECCAN AGENCIES**
4-3-329, Bank Street,
Hyderabad-500195
Ph: 24756967/24756400

**MICRO MEDIA**
Shop No. 5, Mahendra Chambers,
150 DN Rd. Next to Capital Cinema,
V.T. (C.S.T.) Station, MUMBAI-400 001
Ph: 22078296/22078297

**BPB BOOK CENTRE**
376 Old Lajpat Rai Market,
Delhi-110006
Ph: 23861747

Published by Manish Jain for BPB Publications, 20 Ansari Road, Darya Ganj, New Delhi-110002 and Printed by him at Repro India Ltd, Mumbai

www.bpbonline.com

# Dedicated to

*Mum and Dad – for everything*
*Amanda – for all your support and love in the crazy things I do*

# About the Author

 **Paul Battisson** is a 7-time Salesforce MVP, Certified Salesforce Instructor, and has obtained 13 Salesforce certifications to date. He is the COO of Cloud Galacticos, a Salesforce partner in the UK, and runs the popular CloudBites.tv blog and associated YouTube channel with his videos achieving over 100k views. He has been working in the Salesforce ecosystem for over ten years and has experience in several languages and frameworks. He is the author of the course "Astronomical Apex Testing" and has spoken at over 50 different technology events worldwide.

# Acknowledgments

I am very fortunate to have been able to work with a lot of people during my time in the Salesforce ecosystem, who have all made me a much smarter person. Thanks to the team at Cloud Galacticos for being an amazing bunch to work with that keep me on my toes. Phil Walton for friendship, beers, and a job. Neel Meghani for teaching a teenager and still working with him a lifetime later. A particular thanks to Carolina Ruiz, who fielded so many of my dumb questions when I first started working with Salesforce. I can happily say I would never have made it here today without her help and support, you are one of my best friends and an amazing teacher. Kerry Townsend for the great chats and being a sounding board for some of the ideas that lead to this book. Joe Ferraro, Jen Wyher, PK, Dave, and all the other Mavens team that pushed me to be my best during my time there. The many friends throughout the Salesforce world that have taught me a lot. To all my friends and family for your love and support over the years and putting up with me talking about that Salesforce thing. Lastly, thank you to BPB Publications for all the support and cooperation extended throughout for actualizing the project in time.

# Preface

Over the 11+ years I have worked with Salesforce® I have had the pleasure of teaching a number of people how to develop applications using it. I wanted to try and write a book that can help either a point and click admin or developer new to the platform understand from the ground up how to program using Apex. I am a self-taught developer and this book aims to teach you Apex in what I believe is the best way possible given my experience. It is not a rehash of the developer guide but an attempt to provide a clear way to learn the Apex language to build applications on the Salesforce® Platform.

Topics covered in this book include the very basics of working with the platform, and it's the underlying structure, how to define variables and manipulate data, through to triggers, OOP in Apex, and unit testing your code. Each chapter builds on the last, layering on knowledge to help you understand how the pieces of the language interact together and work to produce a complete application. The book also touches on best practices throughout to help the reader start their development on the right foot.

Readers with experience on the Salesforce® Platform will find the early chapters and concepts simpler; however, the book is targeted at any reader wishing to begin working in Apex. Chapters contain example code that covers concepts, with knowledge check questions at the end of the chapter to help reinforce key concepts. Over the book, you will learn the following:

**Chapter 1** introduces the platform and multi-tenant cloud computing paradigm that underpins it. Salesforce's unique database structure and required terminology are covered along with the available tools to a developer, and when they should be used. By the end of the chapter, the reader should have the available knowledge to understand the associated concepts.

**Chapter 2** introduces the Apex programming language and how it compares to other languages that the reader may be familiar with. We discuss the unique elements of the language and how governor limits play a role in thinking about development on Salesforce. We then finish with a discussion of how and when Apex can be executed.

**Chapter 3** guides the reader through defining variables within Apex. This includes the structure of a definition, the primitive data types provided within the language, as well as the concept of sObjects and how to work with them. The chapter finishes with a look at the Data Manipulation Language (DML) provided by Salesforce to allow interaction with the database.

**Chapter 4** builds on chapter 3 by introducing the different types of collection within Apex and how they function. A detailed discussion of when they are best utilized, combined with how they relate to one another, is provided to help the reader make the most appropriate choices.

**Chapter 5** discusses the different control statements within the Apex language to allow developers to build complex logic. The different assignment and calculation operators are discussed before a dive into the various branching logic options available. The chapter finishes with a discussion around the different types of iteration actions that be taken on a collection.

**Chapter 6** introduces the concept of Apex triggers and the Save Order of Execution. Time is spent discussing how triggers operate, and the impacts of different trigger choices before a basic trigger is written using the knowledge that has been learned throughout the book thus far.

**Chapter 7** details the use of the Salesforce Object Query Language, SOQL, and how a developer can utilize this to retrieve desired data from the database. The various filter options are discussed, and a more complex Apex trigger is constructed using this new information.

**Chapter 8** covers the Salesforce Object Search Language, SOSL, in both its usage and comparison to SOQL, discussed in the previous chapter. Time is spent reviewing how the two compare, when to use each, and how to filter and manipulate the records returned from a SOSL search.

**Chapter 9** introduces readers to Apex classes and how a developer can define classes and instantiate objects within the Apex language. How to define member variables, properties, and methods are all covered before a discussion of the correct use of constructors, overloading, and when to use inner classes.

**Chapter 10** gives a detailed overview of how to handle inheritance within Apex to build more dynamic and object-oriented applications. The different inheritance options are discussed along with when they should be utilized by the reader to provide the needed functionality.

**Chapter 11** discusses how to test you Apex code in order to deploy it correctly. Time is spent discussing the format of a test as well as how to setup appropriate test data and assert on actions that have been taken.

**Chapter 12** finishes the book with a discussion on making callouts within Apex to integrate Salesforce with other systems, a common requirement for the modern developer. In this chapter, the reader will interact with a custom web service to see how to make and test varying types of calls to an endpoint.

# Errata

We take immense pride in our work at BPB Publications and follow best practices to ensure the accuracy of our content to provide with an indulging reading experience to our subscribers. Our readers are our mirrors, and we use their inputs to reflect and improve upon human errors if any, occurred during the publishing processes involved. To let us maintain the quality and help us reach out to any readers who might be having difficulties due to any unforeseen errors, please write to us at :

**errata@bpbonline.com**

Your support, suggestions and feedbacks are highly appreciated by the BPB Publications' Family.

Did you know that BPB offers eBook versions of every book published, with PDF and ePub files available? You can upgrade to the eBook version at www.bpbonline.com and as a print book customer, you are entitled to a discount on the eBook copy. Get in touch with us at **business@bpbonline.com** for more details.

At **www.bpbonline.com**, you can also read a collection of free technical articles, sign up for a range of free newsletters, and receive exclusive discounts and offers on BPB books and eBooks.

## BPB is searching for authors like you

If you're interested in becoming an author for BPB, please visit **www.bpbonline.com** and apply today. We have worked with thousands of developers and tech professionals, just like you, to help them share their insight with the global tech community. You can make a general application, apply for a specific hot topic that we are recruiting an author for, or submit your own idea.

The code bundle for the book is also hosted on GitHub at **https://github.com/bpbpublications/Learning-Salesforce-Development-with-Apex**. In case there's an update to the code, it will be updated on the existing GitHub repository.

We also have other code bundles from our rich catalog of books and videos available at **https://github.com/bpbpublications**. Check them out!

## PIRACY

If you come across any illegal copies of our works in any form on the internet, we would be grateful if you would provide us with the location address or website name. Please contact us at **business@bpbonline.com** with a link to the material.

## If you are interested in becoming an author

If there is a topic that you have expertise in, and you are interested in either writing or contributing to a book, please visit **www.bpbonline.com**.

## REVIEWS

Please leave a review. Once you have read and used this book, why not leave a review on the site that you purchased it from? Potential readers can then see and use your unbiased opinion to make purchase decisions, we at BPB can understand what you think about our products, and our authors can see your feedback on their book. Thank you!

For more information about BPB, please visit **www.bpbonline.com**.

# Table of Contents

# CHAPTER 1

# An Introduction to the Salesforce Platform

Let's begin with an introduction to Salesforce and the Salesforce Platform. It is likely that you will have at least some familiarity with Salesforce and the Salesforce Platform (often called **Force.com**), but as this book may be read by a variety of audiences I think it best we cover some base material together. If you have been working with Salesforce for a number of years then you may be able to skip this chapter, but I encourage you to read it as a refresher if nothing else.

## Structure

In this chapter we will cover:

- What a multi-tenant cloud is and what multi-tenancy means
- How the Salesforce database is structured
- What are objects and fields
- The declarative tools available to a Salesforce developer

## Objectives

By the end of this chapter you should:

- Understand what multi-tenancy is and the impact multi-tenancy has on programming

- How the Salesforce database is structured
- What are objects and fields?
- What declarative tools are available to us as Salesforce developers which we can utilize?

# The birth of the cloud

In 1999, at the height of the dot com bubble, Salesforce was born and with it cloud computing. Salesforce was the leader of a new wave of companies that would come to dominate the industry by switching the way in which software was distributed and paid for on its head.

**Software as a Service (SaaS)** was a new way of paying for software whereby you simply paid a monthly fee for each user and the vendor dealt with everything else. No hardware, no installations, regular updates, all dealt with for you. Whereas now this seems commonplace, 20 years ago it was revolutionary.

In order to deliver software in this way, a new computing model was needed and thus the cloud was born. Salesforce, unlike its competition, would not require you to have a server somewhere, they would run the solution for you. But with this new model came the challenge of actually building a solution that could scale in a repeatable and simple fashion, that did not need migration to bigger servers constantly, and that would democratize the underlying resources to allow this scaling.

# Multi-tenancy

Salesforce is different from many other clouds in that it is multi-tenant, that is customers share resources. When cloud computing was first popularized, it was mainly about moving a server out from your office or building, and into another building - you were still paying for the same underlying server hardware somewhere. With multi-tenancy, this was all abstracted away so you didn't have to worry about it.

I like to think of it as renting an apartment instead of buying a house. In an apartment building, there are shared services such as water, electricity, and heating. Each tenant in the building gets access to the same amount of each of these and they don't worry about the underlying pipes and management. This is nice and scalable as almost all apartments follow a standard layout and if anything goes wrong, the landlord deals with it. With a house, you may have access to a greater amount of control for how much heat you get, who supplies everything, and some of the core features of the property, but if something goes wrong, you also have to pay to fix it all. You are in control of everything, including security and maintenance. Now for a house, this may be simple enough and manageable, but for a large scale IT infrastructure, this is not as easy.

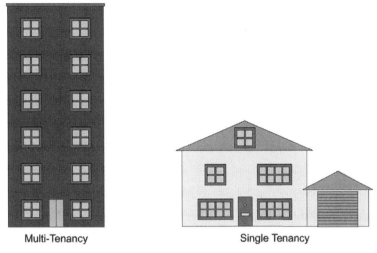

Multi-Tenancy                                                    Single Tenancy

**Figure 1.1:** *Multi vs. single tenancy*

With our apartment, if you need more space, you simply get more space by renting out a bigger apartment. If the landlord upgrades the internet connectivity to the apartment building, everyone gets faster internet.

Whilst multi-tenancy may seem a no-brainier when laid out here, there are some limitations, and on Salesforce these take the form of governor limits. Because the resources are shared, we have to have some rules in place to ensure that one organization does not slow down all of the others. We will discuss this in a lot more detail in the next chapter.

# The Salesforce database

One of the common questions that follow from the idea of multi-tenancy is *does my data live inline with data from other companies?*

The simple answer to this is no. The way in which Salesforce structures the underlying database is one of the many very clever things about Salesforce, and is important for us to understand when we think about how we are writing code, and how our data is both stored and retrieved.

Firstly, each Salesforce organization, or tenant, has a unique OrgID. You can find yours in the **Company Information** section of the **Setup** menu. This unique identifier is used by Salesforce to physically partition the underlying data to both assist in performance but also for querying and scalability. Whenever a query is run in Salesforce, the query engine is targeting a specific tenant's information and so only data within a particular partition is considered.

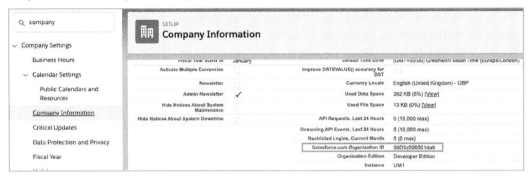

*Figure 1.2: Finding your Organization ID*

The database itself is just a small number of tables that are used to store the metadata for the environment and the data that is being stored. Metadata is data about data, and is used by Salesforce to record the entire structure of our environment. This is one of the reasons that when we create a new object or field in Salesforce that we can quickly add it to the page layout or migrate it between systems, it is simply metadata. Those who have worked with other database solutions know that creating and migrating data structures is a more complex and involved task than it often seems with Salesforce.

# Objects and fields

Now that we understand that Salesforce is not creating tables for us under the hood, we get an insight into why Salesforce has objects and fields instead of tables and columns. Objects and fields in Salesforce are analogous to tables and columns in other databases but importantly are not created as separate tables in the underlying database.

Again, we will see later on how this becomes more important, but for now, we simply need to know that objects in Salesforce are like tables in other database systems and are the entities about which we are storing data, for example, accounts and contacts. Each object in Salesforce has a label such as Job and an API name or developer name. For standard objects, which are those created and maintained by Salesforce, this is simply the same as the label, without spaces, for example, `Account`, `Contact`, `OpportunityProduct`, and `FeedPost`. For custom objects that we define, the `__c` suffix is added to denote it is custom, for example, `Job__c`. The same naming convention is also in place for fields, with standard fields such as `Name` and `LastModifiedDate`, and custom field `Job_Title__c`. Whenever we access an object or field in Apex we need to make sure we use the correct API name.

# Permissions and sharing

Salesforce controls access to data through two mechanisms, permissions, and sharing. Permissions are focussed on what you can do with different objects and follow the standardized **CRUD (Create-Read-Update-Delete)**, model. Permissions are assigned through either a profile or a permission set. Sharing focusses on what records you can see and use these permissions upon. This is a combination of the org-wide default for the object, any inherited sharing through relationships, roles, groups and territories, and then sharing rules and manual sharing.

The reason I bring this up is that Apex runs in system context and will not automatically enforce permissions. This can be extremely useful for us when we want to perform an action that we do not want our users to be able to do on their own, however, care should be taken in certain contexts to ensure that permissions are enforced appropriately. Similarly, Apex can be told to enforce or ignore sharing for a particular user, so when developing our applications we will need to be aware of any inbuilt assumptions we have around whether users should or should not be able to see and or do particular things.

# From clicks to code

We've mentioned a number of declarative features already for Salesforce, and it is outside the scope of this book to cover them all completely, but we should touch on the principle of using clicks and not code within Salesforce whenever reasonable.

One the past few years Salesforce has improved immensely in terms of the power of its declarative automation tools, namely **Flow** and **Process Builder**. These tools have enabled administrators and developers to automate much more rapidly in a way that is easier to maintain. However, these tools are not a panacea, and consideration should always be taken as to when to move from clicks to code.

Code will, in general, always be faster at running a task than an equivalent declarative tool if coded appropriately. For many situations, the performance is so close as to make this difference negligible. However, as volumes grow and complexity increases, the differences become more noticeable and require more thought. As both scale and complexity increase together, code will more than likely become the better choice and make a solution more maintainable.

There are a number of best practices around how to implement and manage your use of declarative tools to help increase a solution's maintainability, scalability, and reliability. Utilizing these practices can help you to move the requirement for code further down the road, but it is unlikely to ever eliminate it completely. Let's look briefly at some declarative tools and when they are unable to be used.

# Workflow Rules

Workflow rules are an extremely powerful engine for you to be able to manage small updates to a record on save. You can also create email alerts, tasks, and send outbound messages. These all operate on a per-record basis and are limited to only being able to update the record in context or records it has a relationship to via lookup or as a detail in amaster-detail relationship. It also has the ability to set certain actions to occur at a specified time. However, you cannot manage records that are not related or child records, and so must use either Process Builder, Flow, or an Apex trigger.

# Process Builder

Process Builder is an abstraction of the Flow automation tool which we will discuss in below, and provides a way for you to define a very specific set of instructions to be reviewed and acted upon in order. Process Builder allows you to update related records in both directions within a record's hierarchy and like workflow, define time-dependent actions. The primary limitations for Process Builder are around bulkification and order of execution.

A best practice is to ensure that for a single object that there is a single Process Builder process defined with all control managed through this one process. In practice, this is not always maintainable and may require the process to be migrated to an Apex trigger. If you find yourself in a situation where you require more than one process per object you should consider migrating these processes to Apex. Process Builder processes have no guaranteed order of execution and so can lead to chained or unexpected results occurring.

# Flow

Flow is a powerful drag and drop programming tool from Salesforce that enables you to draw flow diagrams that Salesforce then interprets into code to run. You can define variables, logic, and loops that enable you to do a lot of simple trigger tasks in a declarative fashion by combining it with Process Builder. You can also create screen flows that define simple to use wizard-style user interfaces.

I am a big fan of Flow for its simplicity and the amount you can do within it. However, performance, bulkification, and manageability are the key areas of concern that will make you think of using Apex code. In many situations, Apex will be more performant than Flow as a developer has hand written code tailored to the desired task – although this is not always true. Flow can be more difficult to modularise and maintain at scale, and as complexity increases. A team will have to think and agree upon a common way of mudlarising and structuring their Flows, something that is a well-solved problem in programming. This also has implications upon the bulkification of data processing, something we will cover in detail in this book for Apex.

# Choose the right tool at the right time

I have listed the declarative tools above in a particular order to illustrate how I view the spectrum of Salesforce automation, as shown below. On the far left, you have the purely declarative and restricted solutions such as formulas, validation rules, and roll-up summary fields. These are all extremely useful tools but do not have a great degree of flexibility. You then move through varying levels of flexibility and ability to handle complexity, from Workflow Rules, then Process Builder, Flow, and finally to Apex.

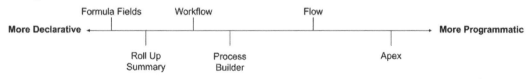

*Figure 1.3:* *The Spectrum of Salesforce Automation*

It is important as a developer that you spend time thinking about what the right tool to use is; you should not view any tool as a hammer and every problem as a nail. When you are starting an implementation with smaller amounts of logic and automation, the declarative tools will allow you to build solutions and solve problems for your users and customers rapidly. As this complexity increases and the scope and scale of the solution grows, you should consider how to move appropriately to a consistent toolset that will allow you to manage this going forward.

# Conclusion

Hopefully, now you have a deeper understanding of how the Salesforce Platform works and some of the considerations you should have in mind when deciding upon a declarative vs. code-based solution. You should always keep declarative features in mind as they can help you in your code immensely (roll-up summaries and formula fields in particular). Let's now start diving into the Apex language and how to develop for the Salesforce Platform using Apex.

# Questions

1. What are some benefits of a multi-tenant vs. a single tenant cloud for developers?
2. What are some drawbacks of a multi-tenant vs. a single tenant cloud for developers?
3. Does Salesforce create new table instances for each new object?
4. What are some of the declarative tools available to us?

# CHAPTER 2

# What is Apex?

This chapter aims to help us understand what Apex is and is not as a programming language, its similarities and differences with other programming languages, and how it can be invoked and executed. We will also spend some time again discussing governor limits, what they are, and how they will impact our thinking.

## Structure

In this chapter we will learn:

- What is Apex?
- The difference between strong and weak typing
- What is an object-oriented programming language?
- How Apex compares to other languages
- What Governor Limits are
- How we can execute Apex
- How we access the developer console and view debug logs

# Objectives

By the end of this chapter you should:

- Understand the attributes of the Apex language and how it compares to other programming languages
- What Governor Limits are and why we need them
- How we can execute Apex
- How to access the Developer Console

# A definition of Apex

The Apex Developers Guide[1] from Salesforce defines Apex as follows:

*Apex is a strongly typed, object-oriented programming language that allows developers to execute flow and transaction control statements on Salesforce servers in conjunction with calls to the API. Using syntax that looks like Java and acts like database stored procedures, Apex enables developers to add business logic to most system events, including button clicks, related record updates, and Visualforce pages. Apex Code can be initiated by Web service requests and from triggers on objects.*

Whilst this is a very comprehensive definition, there are a number of things I want to unpack to help build out our understanding of Apex more deeply.

# Strong and weak typing

A programming language can be described as being strongly or weakly typed. This label refers to the way in which the language deals with variable declaration and data types.

In the snippet below, we see some JavaScript code, which is weakly typed (JavaScript is a weakly typed language):

```
var myVariable = 'Paul';

myVariable = 10;

myVariable = true;
```

This code is completely valid and will run. We define a variable (a placeholder label for some data) called myVariable and assign it 3 different values (the string Paul, the

---

1    https://developer.salesforce.com/docs/atlas.en-us.apexcode.meta/apexcode/apex_intro_what_
     is_apex.htm

number 10, and the boolean value true). Whilst if we were to try and use the data at different points we may get some issues if the data is of the wrong type, there is nothing inherently wrong with this, and is very common with many languages.

Let us now instead consider the snippet of code below which is written in Apex. In it we define a variable called myName, which has a datatype of string - that is a string of alphanumeric characters:

```
String myName = 'Paul';

myName = 10; //This would throw an error on save
```

In the second line, we then try to repeat our previous action of assigning a numerical value to the variable, but instead get an error when we try to save[2]. This is because Apex is a strongly typed language, that is, when we work with data in Apex, we have to know the type of data we are working with. The text after the double forward slash // is a comment and is ignored by the system, allowing us to add useful information to our code for ourselves and other developers.

# Object-oriented programming

When computers were first being programmed, they operated in a very strict fashion on a set of instructions. Instructions would be executed line by line until they reached the final instruction was executed and the program would then terminate. Developers started to include lots of navigation into their programs to allow the code to stay alive once launched to keep it running until the user decided to terminate it.

This worked well for a lot of the initial uses of computer systems, but as more applications were built it became somewhat of a restriction in the way in which these languages would operate. It also became more difficult as developers tried to turn more complex domains into computer programs.

Let's think about defining shapes for a drawing application. We have many different types of shapes such as circles, rectangles, squares, pentagons, and so on. Each of them have some common properties, such as a number of sides and the fact they have a color. They will also have some common actions, for example, drawing a shape starting from an initial set of coordinates and given some parameters.

---

2    The error is technically on compilation, but we will discuss that more later.

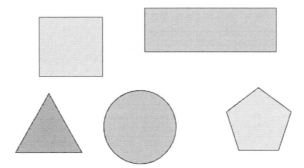

*Figure 2.1: A collection of shapes*

In the non object-oriented view of programming, you would define a different set of functions for each shape and the system would then need to know about what shape it was drawing to allow it to draw the shape. This is fine, but what happens if we want to add a new shape? We then have to add a new shape definition set and make the system aware of it in all the required places. Similarly, if we want them all to have a new property such as opacity.

**Object-oriented programming (OOP)** allows us to think of items we are working with in terms of objects (that is instances) of different types (that is things or concepts). For our shapes, we can think of a circle type, which we can create instances of with different radii.

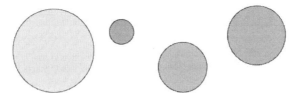

*Figure 2.2: Some circles*

This can be further enhanced with the idea of inheritance which is another key OOP principle. We can define subtypes, which can inherit properties and methods from other types. So we could define a *Shape* type which has some properties such as color and opacity, and a method called draw which would take in a set of parameters and draw the correct shape.

We will discuss inheritance in much more detail later, but for now, it suffices to say that an object-oriented programming language is one where we can define types of data that we can create instances of to work within our solution.

# Apex and other languages

Given that we now have some basic understanding of the structure of Apex, le us now compare it to some other popular languages. Knowing that it is both strongly typed and object-oriented allows us to discuss it relative to those languages most similar to it, namely C# and Java. Whilst other languages will have features that overlap with those of Apex, C#, and Java will be most useful as they are both extremely popular and well known, and the closest to Apex in terms of structure and syntax. In fact, the Salesforce platform itself is written in Java, and Apex is based on Java, hence a lot of the similarities.

Both Java and C# are strongly typed object-oriented languages that enable developers to write applications for deployment anywhere that their respective virtual machines can run. Unlike some other languages, both Java and C# compile into some intermediary code, which is run by a virtual machine that handles dealing with the actual operating system and computer. Apex is similar in that when it is compiled it is to a format that can be interpreted by the Apex runtime interpreter.

Like both C# and Java, Apex also deals with garbage handling and memory allocation for the developer, helping to reduce and minimize errors through memory mismanagement. In terms of syntax it follows a similar structure and for any C# or Java developer reading Apex code should be fairly straightforward given the overlap of common idioms.

The primary difference between the different languages comes from their execution and versioning. Whereas with Java and C# they can both be executed anywhere their virtual machines can run, be that a desktop, a server, the cloud, or mobile phone, Apex can only be executed and run on the Salesforce platform and in the cloud. There is no local compilation and execution of Apex available. This is due to the fact that Apex is firstly multi-tenant aware (i.e. has limits in place to ensure resources are not hogged) and secondly metadata aware. Whenever a new field or object is created in Salesforce, Apex is immediately aware of this new item and can reference it. With all the metadata stored in the Org on the cloud, compiling and executing Apex locally would not enable it to be correctly aware of the Org's metadata.

Apex is also associated with a specific version of the Salesforce API. This allows Salesforce to continue to release new features 3 times a year and update the platform, without breaking existing code on the platform. As a developer, you will need to pay attention to different versions of Apex when using functionality like Dynamic SOQL (which we will cover later in *Chapter 7. SOQL*), but in general code on different versions of the API can happily execute alongside each other and interact.

Another difference between Salesforce and other platforms is the requirement that Apex code deployed to a live production environment must have 75% code coverage from unit tests. We will cover this in more detail in *Chapter 11. Testing Apex*, but it is relevant as we now discuss how we can execute and invoke Apex.

# Executing Apex

As discussed above, Apex can only be compiled and executed on the Salesforce platform. Apex can be invoked or executed in a number of ways, which differ from other programming platforms but have analogous examples and highlight the flexibility of Apex as a programming tool.

# Anonymous blocks

Apex can be executed as an anonymous block of code, that is, a block of code that is merely compiled and executed by the Salesforce platform and not stored as metadata for use at a later date. Anonymous blocks are typically executed through the Execute Anonymous window in the Developer Console, but can also be executed through the API. When you execute an anonymous block, the code is compiled and executed straight away, similar to running an inline script in other languages. Anonymous blocks are extremely helpful for executing single one-off jobs within a solution such as starting a batch job. Unlike other Apex, anonymous blocks do not have a requirement around code coverage, and so will not be tested to the same level as other code executed. For simple processes like starting a batch job, this is fine, but you should avoid running complex anonymous statements wherever possible for this reason.

# Triggers

Triggers in Salesforce are similar to triggers in other database languages and can fire both before and after operations have occurred on records, which are persisted to the database. We will cover triggers and how to use them in *Chapter 6: Apex Triggers*, but for the discussion here it is important to note that you can invoke Apex to run when a record is changed within the system.

# Controllers - Visualforce, Lightning, and JavaScript Remoting

I have grouped all of these as they all are responses to a client-side or web page interaction invoking some Apex code, for example, a button click on a Visualforce page. Although the syntax and ways of invoking the Apex may differ, essentially these all operate the same way to allow communication between the user via a frontend and the Salesforce backend.

# Asynchronous Apex

For longer running tasks that do not need immediate execution, Apex has a number of asynchronous execution options:

- Batch Apex for processing large data volumes.
- Future methods for long-running operations or callouts.
- Queueable Apex for processes that you may want to chain or monitor.
- Scheduled Apex for operations that should fire at a particular time or on a particular date.

All of the above allow you to run Apex code when resources are available for jobs that do not need processing immediately, or cannot be processed immediately due to large volumes.

# Web Services

Apex Code can be exposed as a web service for both SOAP and REST-based APIs that can be called from external systems or using the Salesforce AJAX toolkit. This can allow external applications a far deeper integration with your Salesforce Org and enable you to build out advanced applications that interoperate at scale.

# Email Services

An often-forgotten method for invoking Apex is using the built-in email services capabilities, whereby you can assign Apex classes to handle incoming emails to specific addresses that can be processed to interact with the Salesforce database.

# Saving and compiling Apex

Aside from the anonymous blocks mentioned above, all Apex is saved on the Salesforce platform for execution when invoked in the appropriate manner. When Apex is saved in the form of a class or trigger, it is compiled by Salesforce and stored as metadata on the platform ready for execution. If during this compilation an error occurs then the developer compiling the Apex is informed of the compilation error and must fix the issues before re-attempting compilation. If there is a failure during compilation, the Apex being saved is not updated on the database and the last compiled version (if any) remains.

When an end-user invokes the saved Apex through one of the invocation methods described above, the compiled metadata is retrieved and passed to the Apex interpreter, which executes the Apex for the user. For the end-user, this is all seamless.

# Governor Limits

I want to finish this chapter by spending additional time discussing governor limits, a key feature of Apex that is different from many other platforms. Because Salesforce is a multi-tenant environment, resources have to be shared by users in a consistent way that ensures no one user causes a performance issue for other users on the platform. Salesforce manages this through the use of governor limits.

As we dive deeper into the different sections of this book, we will look at relevant governor limits in detail, but I wanted to cover here why governor limits are a good thing for Salesforce and a good thing for Salesforce developers.

Firstly, and most obviously, governor limits are for the benefit of the entire user base as they restrict the number of resources that anyone user can employ at a time. For all transactions, this allows a certain guarantee of performance as you know that a developer cannot simply execute a method that will hog all of the resources and cause the entire platform to grind to a halt.

For developers, the governor limits are good because they make you consider how you are developing your solution in a way that is going to give your user the best experience possible. Salesforce is a web application on which every interaction for the end-user involves some form of callout from a browser or app to the Salesforce servers. A typical transaction has the following lifecycle:

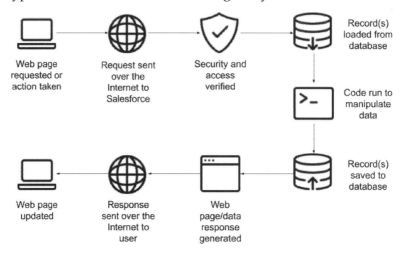

***Figure 2.3:*** *A typical Salesforce transaction lifecycle*

We want to make each of these steps as efficient as possible to ensure the shortest amount of time for the entire lifecycle to complete and the best experience for our end-user. Some of these, such as the user's internet speed for transferring data, are out of our control, but the volume of data we are sending back and forth is. Most importantly for Apex, which is a backend language, the time spent on the Salesforce server executing is under our control through the way in which we architect our application and develop our Apex code. The governor limits are therefore a good way in which Salesforce indirectly enforces a performance requirement on the solutions you build. As a developer, being aware of the governor limits when programming will enable you to produce better code that will scale more readily as the use of your solution grows.

Now we have a good understanding of what Apex is as a language and how we can invoke it, it is time for us to move on to start writing some Apex.

# The Developer Console and debug logs

Before we can begin coding, we need to have a Salesforce environment we can run our code in. We shall use a developer edition environment. You can register for a developer edition for free at https://developer.force.com. Once you have registered and signed in, open the **Developer Console** by selecting the gear icon in the top right of the screen and then clicking **Developer Console** as shown below:

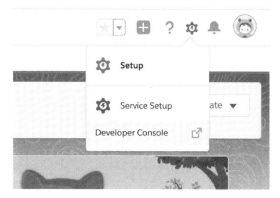

**Figure 2.4:** *Accessing the Developer Console*

The Salesforce Developer Console is a built-in web-based IDE that Salesforce provides to enable developers to write and deploy code to an environment. Launching the Developer Console, you will be presented with a screen as follows:

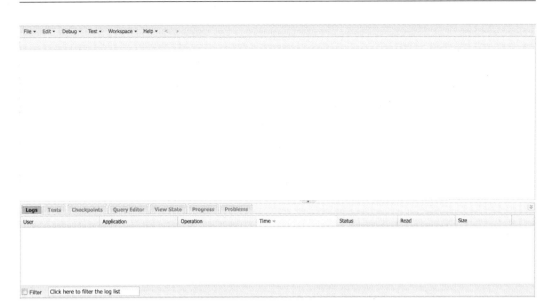

**Figure 2.5:** *The Developer Console*

We will cover different parts of the console as we progress through the book. For now, please select **Debug** from the top menu, then select **Open Execute Anonymous Window**. This will open a small modal window with the title **Enter Apex Code**. This window enables us to enter some code which will then execute as an anonymous block as described above:

**Figure 2.6:** *The Execute Anonymous window*

For *Chapters 3: Variables in Apex* and *Chapter 4: Collections*, we will be seeing how we define variables and collections within Apex, and you can enter the code provided into the Execute Anonymous window to run it and have variables defined. In later chapters, we will also include the `System.debug()` statements. These print out strings of information to the debug log generated when Apex is executed. You can see this in action now by doing the following. In the Execute Anonymous window, enter the following code:

```
System.debug('This is a string of information');
```

Check the checkbox **Open Log** and press execute. You will then be presented with a debug log which roughly halfway down will have the string printed out (as shown in the image below highlighted in blue). If you select the **Debug Only** checkbox, indicated at the bottom of the picture below, the log will filter down to only the debug string we have printed:

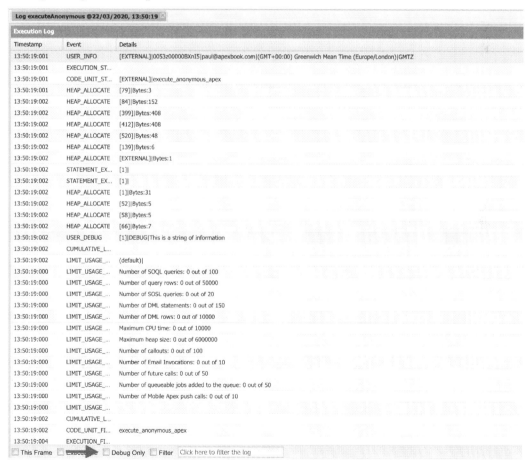

*Figure 2.7: Viewing a debug log*

This will become more useful as we begin running code where we wish to see outputs.

# Conclusion

In this chapter, we have reviewed the Apex language at a high level and seen how it compares to other languages such as C# and Java. We have reviewed the many different ways in which Apex can be invoked, how the governor limits impact upon the way in which we could our Apex and finally run our first piece of Apex through the Execute Anonymous window. Let us continue with learning how to define variables in Apex.

# CHAPTER 3

# Variables in Apex

## Structure

In this chapter we will cover:

- Defining variables in Apex
- Different data types in Apex
- How to create sObject instances
- Working with DML

## Objectives

By the end of this chapter you should:

- Be able to define variables of both primitive and more complex types in Apex
- Be able to create and work with sObject instances
- Know how to manipulate data against the Salesforce database

Variables are the most basic of all programming concepts but are the foundation upon which everything else is built. A variable is a store for some data that can change (or vary) over time. If you have done algebra at school you will be familiar with variables such as x = 5, which is a variable called x whose value is 5. Variables are defined to allow us to hold and manipulate data within the system.

As Apex is a strongly typed language, we have to define the data type for the variable we are instantiating. Salesforce has a number of different data types which we will cover here that behave in different ways. The first and most basic of these data types are known as primitive data typess.

# Primitives

Primitive data types are the foundational data types that are used to hold data we are most familiar with. We define a variable with a primitive data type using the following syntax pattern:

```
DataType variableName = value;
```

It is common practice to use what is called *camel case* in naming your variables in Apex, as shown with `variableName` rather than `variable_name` or another structure. Below we will detail each primitive data type, how to declare a variable in that type and when you might use the type.

# Blob

A `Blob` is a set of binary data stored in a single object, for example, it can be the response from a web services request or the body of an attachment to an email. You can create a `Blob` by either assigning it the value of an attachment or document body, or through converting a string into a `Blob` object as shown below:

```
Blob myDataBlob = Blob.valueOf('my text to convert');
```

`Blob` values are also commonly used in processes where you are either encrypting to a `Blob` or decrypting from a `Blob` to add some additional security to a set of data.

We have also called our first method here, `valueOf()`. In Apex, you call methods on a class using the dot notation, `Blob.valueOf()`, and pass in any parameters between the parentheses. We will cover this in more detail later in *Chapter 9. Apex Classes* where we discuss classes and methods, but it is important here to understand that we are calling the `valueOf` method on the `Blob` class and passing in a string parameter (more on strings below).

# Boolean

`Boolean` values are simple true or false values used for logical processing or holding some state which is either on or off. For example, you may bind a checkbox on a page to a `Boolean` value to store whether that checkbox is checked or not, and default it to false:

```
Boolean isChecked = false;
```

`Boolean` values are also returned by comparison operators which we will discuss in *Chapter 5: Control Statements and Operators*, however, I want to discuss the null value before we continue. In Apex, unlike some other languages, `Boolean` variables can hold 3 different states, `true`, `false`, and `null`. It is a best practice to always declare a `Boolean` to be in either a `true` or `false` state by default rather than leave it to default to `null` as this will cause a `NullPointerException` when attempting to use in in comparisons and your code will fail. We will discuss the `null` value and `NullPointerException` in more detail later in this chapter.

# Date

The `Date` data type stores information on a particular day without holding any information on the time of day. An example of this would be someone's birthdate or the date on which a sales opportunity is expected to close. `Date` and its related primitives, `DateTime`, and `Time` are slightly different from other primitives in that they must be created using a static system method, like `Blob`. We will cover what a static method is in more detail later, but for now, it is only important to know we define a `Date` using the following syntax:

```
Date christmas = Date.newInstance(2020, 12, 25);

Date todaysDate = Date.today();

Date newYearsEve = Date.parse('31/12/2020');
```

We can see here we have defined 3 different dates using 3 different static system methods, `newInstance` which takes in the year, month, and day parameters, `today` which returns today's date, and `parse` which takes in date as some text. You can see here that the date for New Year's Eve is written in the dd/mm/yyyy format used in Europe. This method is contextually aware and will use the user's local date format.

# Datetime

`Datetime` is a primitive holding both a date and a particular time on that date, commonly used for either time-dependent information such as appointment time, or for storing auditing and logging information such as the day and time on which an action occurred. Similar to `Date` you create `Datetime` values using static system methods, the two most common of which from my experience are:

```
Datetime thisMoment = Datetime.now();

Datetime meetingStart = Datetime.newInstance(2020, 9, 1, 9, 30, 0);
```

The first method defines a variable `thisMoment` which is assigned the value of the date and time (including milliseconds) of when that variable is created. The second line defines a variable `meetingStart` that holds the value 9:30 am on the 1st of September 2020.

# Decimal

The `Decimal` data type is used for storing numerical data including decimals, but that have a fixed scale that can either be set explicitly or from the data creating the variable. `Decimal` data is mainly used when dealing with currency fields that will return data in Apex as a decimal.

```
Decimal itemCost = 1.99;

Decimal percentageComplete = 15.266543;
```

The `itemCost` variable has the scale set to 2 decimal places and the `percentageComplete` variable to 6 decimal places. If we are dealing with any sort of calculation where we require specific accuracy, we should use the `Decimal` type, however, it is important to be aware of the scale of the data to avoid rounding errors.

# Double

Similar to `Decimal` is `Double`, again a number involving a decimal point, but in this instance a 64-bit number with a maximum value of $2^{63} -1$ and a minimum value of $-2^{63}$ (that is a value between positive 9 quintillion and negative 9 quintillion (approximately). `Doubles` variables however are not as accurate for storing values as variables of the `Decimal` type and so we should avoid them for any financial calculations.

```
Double goldenRatio = 1.61803398875;
```

# Id

This is a special data type available to Apex and Salesforce programmers, and is the 18 character `Id` for a particular record. Salesforce verifies the `Id` at runtime when a variable of type `Id` is assigned a value and will error if the value is invalid. It will also convert a 15 character `Id` into an 18 character `Id` as part of this process.

```
ID accountId = '0013z00002PNSXtAAP';
```

# Integer

The `Integer` data type can hold any whole number between 2,147,483,647 and -2,147,483,648. `Integers` variables are used a lot as counting variables and in loops to help keep track of progress through a collection.

```
Integer total = 25;
```

# Long

A `Long` value is a very big integer, which is a value without a decimal point between $2^{63} - 1$ and $-2^{63}$ (again between positive and negative 9 quintillions roughly). In my work with Salesforce, I have not come across many instances where I have needed to use the `Long` data type although this just maybe because my numbers haven't been big enough. If you do not need over 2,147,483,647 or less than -2,147,483,648 you should use the `Integer` data type, otherwise, you can define a `Long` in the following way:

```
Long revenue = 3147483647L;
```

# Object

In the last chapter, we discussed what it means for a programming language to be object-oriented . We discussed the fact that it means we can have objects inherit from each other - our circle and our rectangle classes both inherited from our shape class. In what is a bit of a philosophical question, it is right to ask what our shape class inherits from, and for our primitive types what do they inherit from if everything is an object? What came first? The answer is the `Object` data type.

All other data types in Apex, primitives included, inherit from the `Object` data type. You can cast variables of the `Object` data type to a more specific data type as long as the underlying data in that variable is of a compatible type. Casting changes the data from a variable from one type into another compatible data type, for example from an `Integer` to an `Object` or from an `Object` holding compatible data to an `Integer`. You can see an example of declaring a variable of an `Object` data type with `Integer` data and then casting to an `Integer` type variable below:

```
Object myData = 1618;

Integer myIntegerData = (Integer)myData;
```

You cast data between types by placing the new data type in parentheses before the data or name of the variable being cast. The `Object` data type is typically used when you are unsure of the type of data you are receiving, for example in a web service callout before being cast to another data type.

# String

The `String` data type is for any collection of characters enclosed within single quotation marks such as:

```
String myName = 'Paul';

String favouriteIceCream = 'Mint choc chip';

String empty = '';

String greeting = 'Hello ' + myName;
```

In the final variable, we declare a variable called greeting. You can see we are able to concatenate strings together using the + symbol so that greeting has the value `Hello Paul`.

The variable we defined called empty is the `empty` string, which is a string containing no characters with length 0. It is important to note that this is different from `null` which is a string with no characters and not the empty string. We will discuss `null` in more detail below.

You may be wondering how we can include single quotations in our strings given that we enclose the string in single quotations. For certain special characters, we can use escape strings such as:

```
String tab = 'My\ttab string';

//My    tab string

String carriageReturn = 'My\rcarriage return string';

//My

//carriage return string

String lineFeed = 'My\nline feed string';

//My

//line feed string

String singleQuote = 'My\'single quote string\'';

//My'single quote string'

String doubleQuote = 'My\"double-quote string\"';

//My"double-quote string"
```

```
String backslash = 'My\\backslash string';
```

```
//My\backslash string
```

# Time

Our final primitive data type is `Time` which is very similar to `Date` and `DateTime` and represents a timestamp that is not dependent on a day. You define a `Time` type variable using the static `newInstance` method as shown below

```
Time coffeeTime = Time.newInstance(10, 35, 23, 400);
```

This defines the time 10:35:23:400 (10:35 am, 23 seconds, and 400 milliseconds). This method assumes you are using the Coordinated Universal Time (UTC) timezone[1].

# Nulls

What happens if we don't assign any value to a variable - what is its value then? If a variable is declared without a value (or a new object instance) then it will be given the value of `null`. `Null` is a special data type meaning nothing or the absence of data.

People often confuse `null` as meaning 0 or an empty string `' '` but it is different from that and means "something that has no value at all". A way I like to think of this is that I have no sisters, so the number of sisters I have would be the value 0. If you asked me the age in years of my oldest sister, that value would be `null` - there is no value, not even 0. `Null` values are important to be aware of as developers can forget about declaring values and result in a `NullPointerException`.

A `NullPointerException` is one of the most common exceptions seen in Apex and is where you ask the system to perform some action on a value that does not exist i.e. is `null`. Using our example of my none existent sisters, if you wanted to get the month portion of my oldest sister's birthday, you would get a `NullPointerException`, that is we are trying to find the month portion of a date that is non-existent, i.e. `null`.

# Constants

We now understand how to define variables so that we can work with data that might change over time, but how about data that we know is going to stay fixed? An example may the maximum number of items we want to display in a list, or the text for a welcome message. You declare a constant variable in Apex by prefixing the declaration with the keywords `static` `final`. The use of both the `static` and `final`

---

1　UTC is a fixed timezone that does not adjust to daylight savings and is the basis for all time coordination globally.

keywords mans that the constant can only be defined or assigned a value where it is declared or in a static block. We will discuss static blocks in more detail later when discussing classes.

```
static final String GREETING = 'Hello ';

static final Integer MAX_ITEMS = 2000;

static final Double PI = 3.14;
```

You may have noticed that I have named the constants GREETING, MAX_ITEMS, and PI rather than greeting, maxItems, and pi. This a particular naming convention for constants popular in languages like Apex, C#, and Java. It serves no technical purpose (the lowercase names work just as well) but for readability, I would advise following this convention when working with constants.

# sObject, sObjects, and sObject instances

Another property of Apex that we briefly mentioned is that Apex is aware of the metadata within our org - it knows that we have a certain standard and custom objects and fields available to us. In order for us to work with records within Apex Salesforce provide the sObject (Salesforce Object) data type. This is the base data type for any standard or custom object in Salesforce, and from this base type, we get specific instances of object types for our custom and standard objects.

What does this all look like in practice? Let's say we have 2 objects we want to work with, the standard account object and a custom job object. The API or developer name for the account object is Account and for our custom job object is Job__c. To declare variables of this type we then simply use the API name in our definition:

```
Account acc = new Account();

acc.Name = 'Acme';

Job__c job = new Job__c();
```

Let's talk through these 3 lines in some more detail as there are a number of things going on. Firstly, we have the new Account data type being applied to the variable we are defining called acc on the top line, this we have seen before. However, after the = we have newAccount() - what does this mean?

Unlike our primitive data types, Account represents something more complex, an individual account record with our fields on it such as Name. When we are working with account records, and in this instance creating a new account record to work with, we have to tell Salesforce this is a new account record instance. We do this using the keyword new, and adding the parentheses after the word Account. The statement newAccount() tells Apex we want a new blank Account record instance for us to work with.

Because our acc variable has the Account sObject data type we can also access the fields on the account as we do on line 2 with the dot notation - acc.Name gets the Name field (or property) of the acc variable, and we assign the value Acme. On the third and final line, we again define a new record of type Job__c using Job__c job = new Job__c(). We could then access any fields we had on the job record using the same dotnotation as before.

# DML

At this point, we should discuss the **Data Manipulation Language** (**DML**). DML is a series of statements and methods available in Apex that enable a developer to push data changes to the Salesforce database. The following keywords are all reserved (that is cannot be used as variable names), and operate on one or more records.

## Insert

The insert statement saves a new record to the Salesforce database. Note that after the insert is performed the Id field on the record is populated by the system:

```
Contact newContact = new Contact(FirstName = 'Paul', LastName =
'Battisson');

insert newContact;
```

## Update

The update statement saves changes to an existing record to the database, and the record must have the Id field populated.

```
Contact newContact = new Contact(FirstName = 'Paul', LastName =
'Battisson');

insert newContact;

newContact.Email = 'test@test.email.com';

update newContact;
```

# Upsert

The upsert statement requires an external Id field to be populated which the system will use to match on. If a match is found an update is performed, otherwise a new record is inserted as if using the insert statement:

```
Contact newContact = new Contact(FirstName = 'Paul', LastName = 'Battisson',
External_Id_Field__c = 'MyExternalId');

upsert newContact;
```

# Delete

The delete statement removes a record with the given Salesforce Id from the database:

```
Contact newContact = new Contact(FirstName = 'Paul', LastName =
'Battisson');

insert newContact;

delete newContact; //Contact is removed from database
```

# Undelete

The undelete statement restores records from the recycle bin. These records must be queried from the database. The query shown below retrieves a set of deleted contacts from the recycle bin with the LastName field equal to Smith. We will cover queries in detail in *Chapter 7. SOQL*

```
undelete [SELECT Id, LastName FROM Contact WHERE LastName = 'Smith' ALL
ROWS];
```

# Merge

The merge statement merges up to 3 records into a single record and removes the others. The first record provided is the master record into which the others should be merged:

```
Contact newContact = new Contact(FirstName = 'Paul', LastName =
'Battisson');

insert newContact;
```

```
Contact newContact2 = new Contact(FirstName = 'Paul', LastName =
'Battissson');
```

```
insert newContact2;
```

```
merge newContact newContact2;
```

These 6 DML statements enable developers to change data on the Salesforce database and work with sObject instances that have been created or manipulated by our Apex code.

# Enums

The final type we will discuss is enum. An enum allows you to define a preset list of identifiers for this abstract type that can be used. Enums are particularly useful when you have a pre-defined list of values that will not change, for example, days of the week, years of the month, or points on the compass. You define an enum using the enum keyword as the data type and passing a comma-separated list of potential values between curly brackets. For example, to define the points on a compass:

```
enum Direction {NORTH, SOUTH, EAST, WEST};
```

Note that it is customary to capitalize the name of the enum and fully-uppercase the potential values. You can then access a value using the EnumName.VALUE syntax:

```
Direction north = Direction.NORTH;
```

Enums are widely used throughout the Apex system classes to define a prescriptive list of options for things such as logging levels.

# Conclusion

In this chapter, we have learned how we declare variables in Apex and some of the different data types we can have - primitives and sObjects. This is an important first step for us in programming in Apex as variables form the basis of all of our programming. We have also seen how to work with sObject records using DML to manipulate data against the Salesforce database.

We still have some data types to see, but that will come later when we talk about creating our own custom data types. Now that we have an understanding of variables, let's move on to collections, that is multiple variables grouped, and see how we can process them.

# Questions

1. What are some primitive data types?
2. What is the structure for declaring a variable in Apex?
3. How do we create a new sObject instance?
4. What is an enum?
5. What are the different DML keywords/instructions?

# CHAPTER 4
# Collections

## Structure

In this chapter we will cover:

- The different types of collections in Apex
- How the collections relate to each other
- How to define each collection
- When to use each collection

## Objectives

By the end of this chapter you should:

- Know how to define different types of collection with different data types in Apex
- Know when each collection type should be used and the properties of the collection that make it appropriate for the use case

In the previous chapter we discussed the different data types we can have in Apex and how we declare variables of these different types for use. In this chapter, I want to discuss the different types of collections in Apex, when each of them may be useful, and how we can work with them. In general, a collection is any data type where we have more than one value stored together for use. Before we do this, however, I want to discuss why collections are so important in Apex.

# The importance of collections

As we discussed in *Chapter 2: What is Apex?*, there are a number of ways in which we can invoke Apex, but arguably the most common is through a trigger. We are going to cover triggers in much more detail in *Chapter 6: Apex Triggers*, but for now, it is important to note that when dealing with data in a trigger, we need to bulkify our code to deal with batches of 200 records at a time. These batches of records are made available to us in a type of collection called a list, and so knowing how to work with such a collection is going to be very important. How can we iterate over this collection and process the values in it?

In *Chapter 2: What is Apex?*, we also discussed Apex as a language has strictly enforced governor limits which require us to be considerate in how we retrieve and process data. As such, sometimes it will be required to retrieve data and store it in memory for with a unique identifier such as the record Id or Name. This can make it easier for us to perform a single query of all the data we will need for a transaction and then process that in memory, rather than make multiple queries which are computationally more expensive.

These are a couple of the big reasons we will want to work with collections; triggers, and bulkification to avoid governor limits. As we go through the collections in this chapter, I will highlight some of these use cases in more detail.

# Lists

A list in Apex is analogous to an array in other programming languages that is it is an ordered list of items that can be referenced by their index.

An aside, for many readers of this book, the concept or indices and ordering is possibly a new one. Let us think of a list a set of boxes, each of which has a label. That label is a number, and these numbers increase as we move through the boxes. We always start with the first box being labeled 0 and count upwards from there. This makes the rest of our labels the offset from our first box, making it quick and easy for us to retrieve data from the list:

*Figure 4.1: A list is a series of boxes with numbered labels*

Lists can contain any data type, but they must have a defined data type. We declare a list in a similar way to declaring a new sObject:

```
List<datatype> myList = new List<datatype>();
```

We use the `List` keyword and include the datatype for the list in angular brackets `<>` afterward. We then continue our variable definition with the variable name and the equals sign, before the `new` keyword and the `List<datatype>` definition again, followed by a pair of parentheses `()` to create the new list instance. Some list examples could be:

```
List<String> names = new List<String>();

List<Integer> ages = new List<Integer>();

List<Account> accounts = new List<Account>();

List<Job__c> jobs = new List<Job__c>();

List<List<Integer>> grid = new List<List<Integer>>();
```

These all define empty lists of different types. The last item defines a list of lists, allowing us to have multidimensional lists.

In certain circumstances we will know the values of the list and can define them on initialization/definition by swapping the parentheses for a pair of curly braces with a comma-separated list of values as shown below:

```
List<String> compass = new List<String>{'North', 'South', 'East', 'West'};
```

More common is going to be the need for us to add an item to a list, which we can do using the add method:

```
List<String> teamMembers = new List<String>();

teamMembers.add('Gary');

teamMembers.add('Lin');

//List has 2 items - 'Gary' and 'Lin'
```

As discussed in *Chapter 2: What is Apex?*, we call the add method using the dot notation `teamMembers.add()`, however this time we are calling it on the `teamMembers` list instance so that we are adding the item to the `teamMembers` list. We pass in the value we want to add, in this case, `Gary` or `Lin` as a parameter to the method.

How about getting data out from the list? Here is where we want to use our index to allow us to retrieve the value stored within one of our boxes. We can use the shorthand array notation common in other languages to retrieve the value. For example:

```
List<String> compass = new List<String>{'North', 'South', 'East', 'West'};

String n = compass[0]; //Sets n to be 'North'

String s = compass[1]; //Sets s to be 'South'

String e = compass[2]; //Sets e to b 'East'

String w = compass[3]; //Sets w to be 'West'
```

This is an extremely useful shorthand for retrieving data from a list and will come in handy when we look at looping through lists in the next chapter.

The other way in which we can access values by their index is using the get method:

```
List<String> compass = new List<String>{'North', 'South', 'East', 'West'};

String n = compass.get(0); //Sets n to be 'North'

String s = compass.get(1); //Sets s to be 'South'

String e = compass.get(2); //Sets e to b 'East'

String w = compass.get(3); //Sets w to be 'West'
```

Both this block of code and the previous one using the [ ] notation are equivalent, but in practice, developers tend to use the first as it is simpler to understand and is similar to most other languages and thus more familiar.

Let us look at defining another list as follows:

```
List<String> compass = new List<String>();

compass.add('North');

compass.add('South');

compass.add('East');

compass.add('South');

compass.add('West');

compass.add('West');
```

How many items does our list now have in it? The answer is 6, the list is 'North', 'South', 'East', 'South', 'West', 'West'. Lists in Apex have no requirement for uniqueness, they only maintain order. This is handy in some cases, but not in others. Say we were preparing a list of record Ids for us to use in retrieving records from the database. We want the entriesin the list to be unique to help in improving our query performance. What do we use then to allow us to do this?

# Sets

A set is an unordered collection of unique items. Unlike lists, sets are collections of unique elements with no duplicates. You declare a set using the `Set` keyword in a way very similar to that of declaring a list:

```
Set<String> myStringSet = new Set<String>();
```

And again we can initialize with some values if they are known using the curly bracket notation and add items using the `add()` method:

```
Set<String> compassSet = new Set<String>{'North', 'South'};

compassSet.add('East');

compassSet.add('West');
```

Sets do not allow the storing of duplicates, so if we tweaked our earlier code to use a `Set` instead:

```
Set<String> compassSet = new Set<String>();

compassSet.add('North');

compassSet.add('South');

compassSet.add('East');

compassSet.add('South');

compassSet.add('West');

compassSet.add('West');
```

The size of the set would remain at 4, `'North'`, `'South'`, `'East'`, `'West'` as those are the only unique values.

Another difference between sets and lists is that you cannot access elements in a set using an index. When working with sets, it is usually to create a unique collection of elements for use in a filter for a query. You can check to see if the set contains a specific element using the `contains` method that returns a Boolean value:

```
Set<String> names = new Set<String>{'Paul', 'Amanda'};

Boolean hasPaul = names.contains('Paul'); //true

Boolean hasAmanda = names.contains('Amanda'); //true

Boolean hasSophie = names.contains('Sophie'); //false
```

It is also common to compare whether a set contains another list or set:

```
Set<String> names = new Set<String>{'Eddie', 'Penny', 'Lila'};

Set<String> names1 = new Set<String>{'Eddie', 'Penny'};

List<String> names2 = new List<String>{'Lila', 'Penny', 'Suzie'};

names.containsAll(names1); //true

names.containsAll(names2); //false
```

When we first started discussing lists we thought of the list as a collection of boxes with numbered labels that were our indices. What if instead of our labels being integers in order we instead wanted to use another piece of data, for example a string? In that case we want to use a map.

# Maps

Maps are a collection of key-value pairs that allow us to store a variety of data types using a key of any data type rather than an integer as an index. For example, say we wanted to store a list of the number of employees for some accounts but wanted to be able to retrieve an account's number of employees from that list using the account's name further on down in our code. This is an ideal situation to use a map. If we wanted to refer back to our box diagram from earlier, it would now be updated to look something like this:

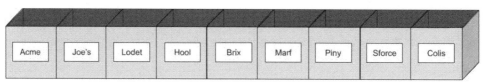

*Figure 4.2: A map is a series of boxes with any label, not just integers*

We declare a map using the Map keyword and placing 2 parameters into the angular brackets rather than a single parameter as we would for a List or a Set. The first is the data type of the keys and the second the data type for the values:

```
Map<keyType, valueType> mapName = new Map<keyType, valueType>();
```

We can use any data type for both the keys and the values. For our example above where we wanted to create a map where we used the name of the account as the key and the number of employees for an account as a value, we would define this map as follows:

```
Map<String, Integer> employeesByAccName = new Map<String, Integer>();
```

To add values to a map you use the `put` method which takes in 2 parameters, the key-value you wish to populate and the value you wish to associate with that key:

```
employeesByAccName.put('Acme', 1000);

employeesByAccName.put('Brix', 550);
```

This code associates the value `1000` with the key `Acme` and the value `550` with the key `Brix`. To retrieve the value for a key from the map we then use the get method for the map which takes in the key-value as a single parameter and returns the value from the map if it exists, and returns `null` otherwise:

```
Integer acmeEmployees = employeesByAccName.get('Acme'); //1000

Integer brixEmployees = employeesByAccName.get('Brix'); //500

Integer testEmployees = employeesByAccName.get('Test'); //null
```

A common issue new developers encounter is attempting to work with an object they have retrieved from a map when it has returned `null` as no value exists. For example, say we had the following code:

```
Map<String, Account> accountMap = new Map<String, Account>

    {

        'Acme' => acmeAccountInstance,

        'Brix' => brixAccountInstance

    };

Integer testEmployees = accountMap.get('Test').NumberOfEmployees;
```

Firstly, we can also use our curly brace syntax on maps to define a map with some values. The *fat arrow* => details which value should be assigned to a particular key. We then attempt to set the value of `testEmployees` as the value of the `NumberOfEmployees` field on the account we retrieve from the map with the key `Test`. However, as there is no value for that key, it will return `null` and an exception will be thrown.

A better way to write this code would be to firstly check to see whether a value exists for the specific key and then if so, set our variable, otherwise set it to a default value. To check whether a key exists within the map, we can use the `containsKey()` method which takes in the key-value as a parameter and returns a Boolean indicating whether the map contains the key. For example:

```
Map<String, Account> accountMap = new Map<String, Account>

    {
```

```
    'Acme' => acmeAccountInstance,

    'Brix' => brixAccountInstance

};
```

```
Boolean containsTestKey = accountMap.containsKey('Test'); //false
```

The keys within our map must be unique, that is each key can only have one value of the specified type and calling put() using the same key multiple times will overwriting the key's existing value.

```
Map<String, Integer> ageMap = new Map<String, Integer>();

ageMap.put('John', 23);

ageMap.put('Jane', 45);

ageMap.put('John', 64);

ageMap.get('John'); //returns 64
```

The same is not true for values within a map though, values do not have a uniqueness requirement.

```
Map<String, Integer> ageMap = new Map<String, Integer>();

ageMap.put('Fred', 29);

ageMap.put('Barney', 30);

ageMap.put('Wilma', 29);

ageMap.put('Betty', 28);
```

This leads us to an interesting observation. The keys of a map are a unique collection with a defined data type, and the values of a map are not a unique collection. From our knowledge of sets and lists, we may then guess that the keys for a map are a set and the values are a list, and our guess would be correct. We can retrieve a set of the keys using the keySet() method and a list of values using the values() method:

```
Map<String, Integer> ageMap = new Map<String, Integer>();

ageMap.put('Fred', 29);

ageMap.put('Barney', 30);

ageMap.put('Wilma', 29);

ageMap.put('Betty', 28);
```

```
Set<String> names = ageMap.keySet(); // Fred, Barney, Wilma, Betty

List<Integer> ages = ageMap.values(); // 29, 30, 29, 28
```

The final example I want to show here with maps is a common pattern for dealing with child records. Often when processing data you will want to retrieve a list of child records for a particular parent record, for example, contacts associated to a particular account. In this instance, it is wise to retrieve all the contacts for the relevant accounts and then to place them in a map where the value data type is a list. For example:

```
Map<Id, List<Contact>> accIdToContactMap = new Map<Id, List<Contact>>();

accIdToContactMap.put(acmeAccount.Id, acmeAccount.Contacts);

accIdToContactMap.put(brixAccount.Id, brixAccount.Contacts);
```

The above code creates a map where the value is a list of contact records, and the keys are account record Ids. One nice piece of syntax that Apex gives us is the ability to refer to related child objects using the relationship name we define, in the case of the standard account-contact relationship is `account.Contacts`. We will cover this in more detail later but for now it suffices to know that this returns a list of contact records. After doing this we could then retrieve the contacts for a particular account later in our code using the `get()` method with an account's Id.

# Conclusion

In this chapter, we have learned what the three different types of collection in Apex are and how we can instantiate and use them. This covers off how we can create and work with the standard types of data that Salesforce provides us. In later chapters, we will see how we can create our custom Apex data types and use them in the same way as the primitives we have defined, and how to work with them in collections. Before we move onto that, however, it is time to learn about control statements within Apex and how we can start working with our data to make decisions.

# Questions

1. What are the three types of collection in Apex?
2. What is the primary difference between a set and a list?
3. What is the difference between a list and a map?
4. What type of collection are the keys of a map?
5. What type of collection are the values of a map?

# Chapter 5

# Control Statements and Operators

So far we have focused on creating variables and collections of variables in Apex to hold our data for us to work with it. In this chapter, we will go through the various control flow statements available to us that will allow us to work with and manipulate our data to control our program flow. By the end of this chapter, we will be aware of the different ways in which we can work with our data, and from there can start developing some examples in Apex bringing this all together.

## Structure

In this chapter we will cover:

- The different control statements available in Apex
- How we can implement comparative and Boolean logic in Apex
- How we can implement different assignment actions in Apex
- How we can perform arithmetic calculations in Apex
- How to create branching logic
- What the `switch` statement is and how to use it
- The different looping options available in Apex

# Objectives

By the end of this chapter you should:

- How to perform different logical operations in Apex
- How to use an `if-else` statement
- How to use a `switch` statement
- How to use the different loop options available in Apex

# Operators

The first thing we will want to look at is our operators, of which there are a number of different types. Below we will see all these operators grouped by type, although it is worth knowing that this is not an exhaustive list (which can be found in the Apex developer documentation), and the groupings are my way of grouping them.

# Comparison operators

Comparison operators, as the name suggests, deal with the process of comparing two values and return a Boolean value that indicates whether the comparison was true or false. The most commonly used comparison operators are as follows.

# Equality ==

The double equals symbol compares whether two values are equal, for example:

```
Boolean equal = 'John' == 'John'; //true

Boolean notEqual = 5 == 4; //false
```

In the above code the values on the left and right of the == are compared and if they are equal `true` is returned, otherwise `false`.

It should be noted that the comparison is by value and not by reference. So we are not checking that it is the same instance of a variable in memory, only that the variables have the same value, unless dealing with a user-defined type. This is a minor point for you to consider and for most developers will not need to be a concern, however, it is something you should be aware of.

# Inequality !=

The inequality operator is the reverse of the equality operator above and compares two values to make sure that they differ:

```
Boolean notEqual = 'John' != 'Michelle'; //true

Boolean equal = 6 != 6; //false
```

# Greater Than >

This operator compares two values and returns true if the left-hand value is larger than the right hand one:

```
Boolean greater = 125 > 4; //true

Boolean notGreater = 6 > 9; //false

Boolean greaterEqual = 7 > 7; //false
```

# Greater Than or Equal To >=

Similarly to the previous greater than the operator, this will return true if the left-hand value is greater than or equal to the right-hand value:

```
Boolean greater = 125 >= 4; //true

Boolean notGreater = 6 >= 9; //false

Boolean greaterEqual = 7 >= 7; //true
```

# Less Than <

This is the reverse of the grater than the operator and returns true if the left-hand side is smaller than the right-hand side:

```
Boolean less = 12 < 20; //true

Boolean notLess = 9 < 7; //false

Boolean lessEqual = 5 < 5; //false
```

# Less Than or Equal To

Again, similar to the previous less than operator but returns true if the left-hand side is less than or equal to the right hand side value:

```
Boolean less = 12 <= 20; //true

Boolean notLess = 9 <= 7; //false

Boolean lessEqual = 5 <= 5; //true
```

# Logical operators

Logical operators allow us to apply Boolean logic to combine multiple Boolean inputs to obtain a single Boolean output. There are three logical operators in Apex, AND, OR and NOT.

## AND operator &&

The double ampersand `&&` AND logical operator will return `true` if both the left-hand side and right-hand side are `true`. The operator will *short-circuit* so that if the left-hand value is `false`, the right-hand value will not be evaluated:

```
Boolean bothTrue = true && true; //true

Boolean rightTrue = false && true; //false

Boolean leftTrue = true && false; //false

Boolean bothFalse = false && false; //false
```

## OR operator

The double pipe[1] `||` OR logical operator will return a `true` value if either the left or the right-hand side are `true`. For the operator to return `false`, both the left and right-hand values must be `false`:

```
Boolean bothTrue = true && true; //true

Boolean rightTrue = false && true; //true

Boolean leftTrue = true && false; //true

Boolean bothFalse = false && false; //false
```

## Not operator ! (logical complement)

The "not" (sometimes called logical complement) operator, returns the inverse value for a `Boolean` variable:

```
Boolean x = true;

Boolean y = !x; //y set to false
```

---

1   The pipe symbol is on the same key as the backslash for English keyboards and can be accessed through Shift + .

# Assignment operators

Assignment operators allow us to assign and set values of variables. We have already seen the basic = operator that sets a variable to the value following the equals sign. We have some additional operators we can use to manipulate values as we assign them.

# Addition assignment +=

The addition assignment operator will take the value on the right-hand side of the operator, add it to the left-hand side before assigning the new total to the variable on the left-hand side. For example:

```
Integer x = 5;

x += 7; //x set to 12
```

If the variable is of type String, we can append another String onto the end using the operator as shown below:

```
String greeting = 'Hello ';

greeting += 'world'; //greeting is now 'Hello world'
```

# Subtraction assignment -=

The subtraction assignment operator is similar to the addition operator in action but subtracts instead of adds the value on the right-hand side:

```
Integer x = 9;

x -= 5; //x set to 4
```

# Multiplicative assignment *=

Multiplicative assignment works in the same way as both the additive and subtractive assignment but multiplies the left and right-hand sides before assigning the total as the new value:

```
Integer x = 12;

x *= 7; //x set to 84
```

# Divisive assignment /=

The final assignment operator we will look at is the divisive assignment operator which divides the left-hand side by the right and then assigns the new value:

```
Integer x = 8;

x /= 4; //x set to 2
```

# Action operators

Action operators take values and act upon them to provide a new value. They are used commonly for mathematical and string operations to help either provide an output or as part of our control statements.

## Addition operator +

The addition operator takes two values and adds them together based upon a number of rules depending on the data type of the values. For `Integer` and `Double` data types, the values are summed:

```
Integer x = 7 + 5; //x set to 12

Double y = 2.4 + 3.2; //y set to 5.6
```

If the first value is a `Date` and the second is an `Integer`, the `Date` is incremented by the number of days specified:

```
Date threeDaysLater = Date.today() + 3; //will set to today's date plus
3 days
```

If the first value is of type `Datetime` and the second is an `Integer` or `Double` then the `Datetime` will be incremented by that number of days (with any decimal portion being the portion of a day):

```
DateTime twoAndAHalfDaysLater = DateTime.now() + 2.5; //will set to 2.5
days (60 hours) later
```

Finally, if two strings are used, the values will be concatenated together to produce a third-string:

```
String helloWorld = 'Hello ' + 'world!'; //et to 'Hello world!'
```

## Subtraction operator -

The subtraction operator works similarly to the addition operator for data of type `Integer`, `Double`, `Date`, and `datetime` as described for the addition operator:

```
Integer x = 9 - 5; //x set to 4

Double y = 12.4 - 3.3; //y set to 9.1
```

```
Date yesterday = Date.today() - 1;

DateTime twelveHoursAgo = DateTime.now() - 0.5;
```

There is no subtraction operator usage on String values.

# Multiplication operator *

The multiplication operator multiplies two values together (which must be of type Integer or Double) and returns the result:

```
Integer x = 3 * 4; //12

Double y = 9 * 0.5; //4.5
```

# Division operator /

The division operator works in the same way as the multiplication operator but divides the first value by the second:

```
Integer x = 20 / 4; //5

Double y = 5 / 2; //2.5
```

# Increment operator

The increment operator will increase the value of a variable by one. This is extremely useful in looping as we will see later:

```
Integer x = 5;

x++; //x set to 6

++x; //x set to 7 - note this syntax is valid but uncommon
```

# Decrement operator --

The decrement operator is the reverse of the increment operator and reduces the value of a variable by one:

```
Integer x = 9;

x--; //x set to 8

--x; //x set to 7 - note this syntax is valid but uncommon
```

## Unary Negation operator -

The unary negation operator takes the value of a variable and multiplies it by -1 turning a negative value positive and a positive value negative:

```
Integer x = 9;

Integer y = -x; //y set to -9
```

Note that if you wanted to inverse the value of a variable and assign the new value to the variable, the following code is equivalent:

```
Integer x = 9;

x = -x; //x set to -9

Integer y = 8;

y *= -1; //y set to -8
```

Whilst both pieces of code are equivalent, the first used on variable x is more commonplace as it is easier to read and understand at a glance what is occurring.

# The if and if-else statements

Now that we have an understanding of the different operators and operations we can apply to our variables, we should look at how we make decisions based upon these values using the operators.

The most common of these is the `if` statement. An `if` statement takes in a `Boolean` value or an expression returning a `Boolean` value, and if that value is `true` will then execute a code block that follows the statement. The format is as follows:

```
if(someBooleanIsTrue) {

//Do something

}
```

The curly brackets here denote the start and end of the code block that we wish to execute should the `Boolean` value evaluate to `true`. An example is:

```
String name = 'Paul';

String greeting = '';

if(name != null) {

    greeting = 'Hello ' + name;
```

```
}
```

```
System.debug(greeting); //prints 'Hello Paul'
```

It should be noted that for single line code blocks after an `if` statement as shown above, the curly brackets are not necessary and the following code would execute and produce the same result:

```
String name = 'Paul';
```

```
String greeting = '';
```

```
if(name != null)
```

```
greeting = 'Hello ' + name;
```

```
System.debug(greeting); //prints 'Hello Paul'
```

My advice to all developers however is to always use the curly brackets as they make your code much more readable to other developers and will ensure your code is understandable should it be passed between machines where indentation may differ.

We can extend our `if` statements using the optional `else` control statement. The `else` statement provides a block of code to be executed should the `Boolean` expression evaluated in the `if` statement return `false`. For example:

```
String name = null;
```

```
String greeting = 'Hello ';
```

```
if(name != null) {
```

```
greeting += name;
```

```
} else {
```

```
greeting += 'stranger';
```

```
}
```

```
System.debug(greeting); //prints 'Hello stranger'
```

We can also chain repeated `else if` statements together to enable us to have multiple branches:

```
//previous code has provided us with an account sObject instance in the
variable acc
```

```
String orgSize = '';
```

```
if(acc.NumberOfEmployees <= 50) {

orgSize = 'Small';

} else if(acc.NumberOfEmployees <= 250) {

orgSize = 'Medium';

} else if(acc.NumberOfEmployees <= 1000) {

orgSize = 'Large';

} else {

orgSize = 'Enterprise';

}
```

We can also nest `if` statements within each other to add complex decision-making flows. If we wanted to analyze our account from before further to highlight small businesses with a high revenue per employee to invest in, we could use a nested `if` statement as shown below:

```
//previous code has provided us with an account sobject instance in the
variable acc

String orgSize = '';

Boolean investmentTarget = false;

if(acc.NumberOfEmployees <= 50) {

orgSize = 'Small';

if(acc.AnnualRevenue/acc.NumberOfEmployees > 1000000) {

investmentTarget = true;

}


} else if(acc.NumberOfEmployees <= 250) {

orgSize = 'Medium';

} else if(acc.NumberOfEmployees <= 1000) {

orgSize = 'Large';

} else {
```

```
orgSize = 'Enterprise';

}
```

In the above code, we can see that should a small company have revenue larger than $1,000,000 per employee we would set the `investmentTarget` `Boolean` to `true`.

`If-else` conditional statements form the basis of most program flow within Salesforce and allow you to build complex decision trees to control the logic and flow of your programs. There is one final type of `if-else` expression to cover before we move on, which is the ternary-if statement.

# Ternary-if

The word ternary is a mathematical term meaning *composed of three parts* and this gives us a hint to the structure of a ternary-if statement. Ternary-if statements are single line expressions that assign a value based upon a decision made inline. A ternary if is formed of three parts:

```
variable = booleanExpressionToEvaluate ? outcomeIfTrue : outcomeIfFalse;
```

Let us take one of our earlier `if-else` statements:

```
if(name != null) {

greeting += name;

} else {

greeting += 'stranger';

}
```

This `if-else` statement has a simple set of defined outcomes, either we append the value in the `name` variable if it has a value, or the string `stranger` if it has none. Because of this, we could rewrite this using a ternary-if statement as follows:

```
greeting += name == null ? 'stranger' : name;
```

Our three parts are then as follows; `Boolean ExpressionToEvaluate` is `name == null`, this will return true if the name variable is `null` and `false` otherwise (it is the inverse of the original logic to make it easier to read). If the name is `null`, we return the string `stranger` to append to the greeting, otherwise, we append the value of the `name` variable.

Ternary-if statements can be extremely useful when working with simple `if-else` statements, however, you should always keep readability of your code in mind when developing. Although you can nest ternary-if statements your code will rapidly become difficult to read and understand for the next developer working on it.

# Switch statements

The `switch` statement allows you to evaluate a variable and execute a block of code based upon the value of the variable matching a defined value. The standard format for a `switch` statement is:

```
switch on variable {

when value {

//Code to execute

}

}
```

An example is:

```
//Integer i defined previously with a value

switch on i {

when 1 {

System.debug('This is the number one');

}

when 2 {

System.debug('This is the number two');

}

}
```

You can also provide a comma-separated list of values to match instead of just individual values. In the example below, we are taking an `Integer` and depending on its value printing to the debug logs whether it is even or odd:

```
//Integer i defined previously with a value

switch on i {

when 0, 2, 4, 6, 8 {

System.debug('This is an even number');
```

```
}

when 1, 3, 5, 7, 9 {

System.debug('This is an odd number');

}

}
```

As we can see from this code, it will work well for integers less than 10 but fails at that point. We can provide a default option with a when else clause:

```
//Integer i defined previously with a value

switch on i {

when 0, 2, 4, 6, 8 {

System.debug('This is an even number');

}

when 1, 3, 5, 7, 9 {

System.debug('This is an odd number');

}

when else {

System.debug('You need to have an integer less than 10');

}

}
```

This final statement will be executed should the variable fail to meet any of the previous criteria. It should also be noted that null is considered a legitimate value and should be handled as such:

```
//Integer i defined previously with a value

switch on i {

when 0, 2, 4, 6, 8 {

System.debug('This is an even number');

}
```

```
when 1, 3, 5, 7, 9 {

System.debug('This is an odd number');

}

when null {

System.debug('No number has been provided');

}

when else {

System.debug('You need to have an integer less than 10');

}

}
```

We can see here that the when null clause has been inserted before the when else. This is because switch statements do not follow through or cascade, once a when clause has been executed the switch statement exits. Because of this, we should always have the whenelse clause as the final clause in the switch statement.

We can also use the return from a method call instead of a variable for our input to the switch statement:

```
switch on getSomeNumber() {

when 0, 2, 4, 6, 8 {

System.debug('This is an even number');

}

when 1, 3, 5, 7, 9 {

System.debug('This is an odd number');

}

when null {

System.debug('No number has been provided');

}

when else {

System.debug('You need to have an integer less than 10');
```

```
}
```

```
}
```

One of the most powerful features of the switch statement is the ability to switch on the type of an sObject record to enable you to cast objects appropriately. This will be extremely useful later when we discuss SOSL in *Chapter 8: SOSL*. An example is shown below:

```
switch on sObjectInstance {
```

```
when Account acc {
```

```
System.debug('This is an account');
```

```
}
```

```
when Job__c job {
```

```
System.debug('This is a job');
```

```
}
```

```
}
```

This allows us to take an unknown sObject record instance sObjectInstance and dependent upon its type have it implicitly cast and available for manipulation.

We can also use the switch statement with enum values for the when clauses:

```
enum Direction {NORTH, SOUTH, EAST, WEST};
```

```
Direction direction = Direction.EAST;
```

```
switch on direction {
```

```
when Direction.NORTH {
```

```
System.debug('Heading north');
```

```
}
```

```
when Direction.SOUTH {
```

```
System.debug('Due south');
```

```
}
```

```
when Direction.EAST {
```

```
System.debug('Travelling east');
```

```
}

when Direction.WEST {

System.debug('Out west');

}

}
```

# The do-while loops

A do-while loop allows a developer to specify a block of code that they want to execute whilst a set Boolean condition remains true. The structure of a do-while loop is as follows:

```
do {

//Block of code to execute

} while(booleanCondition);
```

For example, if we wanted to run a loop that summed the amount field for a set of 10 opportunity records from a larger list, we could use a do-while loop as shown below:

```
Integer i = 0;

Decimal total = 0.00;

do {

total += oppList[i].Amount;

i++;

} while(i < 9);
```

It is important to note that a do-while loop will always execute at least once as the Boolean condition is not checked until after the do block has been executed for the first time. If we require the condition to be checked first then we should use a while loop instead.

# The while loop

The while loop is similar to a do-while loop in that it evaluates a code block whilst a Boolean condition is met, however, in a while loop the condition is evaluated before the code is executed. The format for a while loop is:

```
while(booleanCondition) {

//Code to execute

}
```

If we took our previous example code written in the do-while format and updated it for a while loop it would look as follows:

```
Integer i = 0;

Decimal total = 0.00;

while(i <= 9) {

total += oppList[i].Amount;

i++;

}
```

Note here that we have updated the Boolean condition to be i <= 9 to capture the instance where i is equal to 9.

# For loops

For loops are the third looping option within Apex, and the most commonly used as they are used extensively in Apex Triggers which we will cover in the next chapter.

For loops can be constructed in a number of ways. The format most familiar to those who have worked with other programming languages will be as follows:

```
for(Integer i = 0; i < limitValue; i++) {

//Execute some code i times

}
```

The most common structure for this is to use the size() method on a list to retrieve the total number of elements in the list, and then iterate over them, for example:

```
List<String> letters = new List<String>{'a','b','c','d','e'};

for(Integer i = 0; i < letters.size(); i++) {

System.debug(letter[i]);  //Prints 'a','b','c','d','e' to debug log
individually

}
```

It should be noted that it is a common programming convention to use i as the counter variable here, although any letter can be used.

The second variation of a for loop is to utilize a List or Set of items and iterate over them directly:

```
for(DataType variableName : List<DataType>) {

//Execute code

}
```

```
for(DataType variableName : Set<DataType>) {

//Execute code

}
```

Here the variable variableName must have the same data type as the List or Set. With our earlier example:

```
List<String> letters = new List<String>{'a','b','c','d','e'};

for(String letter : letters) {

System.debug(letter);    //Prints  'a','b','c','d','e'  to  debug  log
individually

}
```

This syntax is slightly easier to read and also provides us a named variable, in this case called letter, that holds the data for the current iteration of the loop. Note however that the variable is unavailable outside the loop context.

As a for loop can iterate over a list of any data type, we can also iterate over loops of sObjects. This can either be done just as above:

```
for(Account acc : accList) { //accList has type List<Account>

System.debug(acc.Name); //Prints the Name of each account

}
```

Another way of retrieving a list of sObject instances is to use a SOQL query to retrieve data from the database. We are going to dive into SOQL in more detail in *Chapter 7: SOQL,* but for our discussion here it is important to know that a SOQL query returns a list of the sObject type, for example, the query [SELECT Id, Name FROM Account] will return data with the type List<Account> and for each Account record will have 2 fields, the `Name` and the `Id`. We can, therefore, use this list in a loop as follows:

```
for(Account acc : [SELECT Id, Name FROM Account]) {

System.debug(acc.Name);

}
```

# Conclusion

We have now covered how to control the flow of different parts of our application with code. Using these different options will allow us to actually make the various decisions and logic steps our code will need to act as desired. We will start to build out some real-world examples in the next chapter on triggers.

# Questions

1. How do we compare whether a value is larger than or equal to another?
2. What do the following logical operators do?
   a. OR
   b. AND
   c. NOT
3. What does an `if` statement do?
4. What is the difference between the `do-while` and `while` statements?
5. What does a `for` loop allow us to do?

# CHAPTER 6

# Apex Triggers

## Structure

In this chapter we will cover:

- What is an Apex trigger?
- The different types of Apex trigger
- The Save Order of Execution
- When to use each trigger type and the context variables available to them
- How to write a trigger
- How to bulkify a trigger

## Objectives

By the end of this chapter you should:

- Be able to define an Apex trigger
- Know how to correctly bulkify a trigger
- Know the different trigger types and when to use them
- Know the different trigger context variables and how to use them.

Up until this point, a lot of the code we have seen has been merely example code to show how a particular feature or aspect of the language functions. From this point on all the code we write will be for a real-world use case. You can take this code and deploy it to a standard Salesforce developer org which you can get for free at developer.salesforce.com/signup. In order to write and save the code, we will use the Salesforce developer console. Once you are logged into your org, click the gear icon in the top right and select **Developer Console**.

# What is an Apex trigger?

When working with a database, we will sometimes want to perform certain actions whenever a record is being changed against the database. For example, in the last chapter, we saw some example code where we wanted to set the size of the company based upon the number of employees that the company had. We want this to occur every time a new account record is saved, and so is something we would place in a trigger.

Triggers are special bundles of code that fire whenever an appropriate database action occurs. We can use triggers to allow us to define complex logical processes that occur whenever a record is changed against the Salesforce database.

## Triggers vs. Workflow/Process Builder

Salesforce contains a number of different automation tools including Workflows and Process Builder that also fire on save and allow you to set criteria for them to run. You can think of both Workflow and Process Builder as visual ways of declaring an Apex trigger - you can do the same actions in a code based trigger, but it is often easier to use a Workflow or Process Builder, especially for point and click developers or administrators.

As a developer, you should always review all of your options before writing any code. The example code I referred to where we set the organization size based upon the number of employees could be done using a formula field. This would be easier to maintain, deploy, and manage in the long term and so is the correct solution.

We should look to use a trigger-based solution when complex logic is involved that either cannot be done in a Process Builder/Workflow, or requires the manipulation of data across multiple disparate objects. As we discussed previously, it is a best practice for you to maintain a single Process Builder per object. If you find that you are requiring multiple overlapping Process Builders to enable your solution to operate, this would be a good candidate for migrating the existing processes to a single trigger. Finally, triggers can fire on deletion and undeletion of records as we shall see shortly, which is not possible for a declarative tool.

# Types of Apex Trigger

Triggers in Apex fire in a number of different contexts. Broadly speaking, I classify triggers into 2 contexts and 4 types. The 4 types of the trigger are as follows:

- insert–runs when creating a new record.
- update–runs when updating an existing record.
- delete–runs when removing a record.
- undelete–runs when reinstating a record from the recycle bin.

A trigger can either run in a before context or an after context. The before and after here refer to the record being saved against the database, and in the case of a record being inserted, it receiving an Id. Note that not all trigger types can run in both contexts. The table below highlights which contexts are available to which trigger type.

| | | Context | |
| --- | --- | --- | --- |
| | | Before | After |
| Trigger Type | Insert | ✓ | ✓ |
| | Update | ✓ | ✓ |
| | Delete | ✓ | ✓ |
| | Undelete | ✗ | ✓ |

*Table 6.1*

The combination of these contexts and types gives us a flexible framework with which we can create and manage repeatable changes and logic that we want to apply to our records as they enter and move throughout various states within the system. Again, it is worth reflecting on the fact that Salesforce is a transactional system, and as such triggers will be a primary focus point for a lot of our code-based development.

Within our system we will use a combination of the various trigger types and contexts - dependent upon the logic we wish to run or outcome we wish to obtain. In order for us to more clearly understand how to make that decision, we should first review the save order of execution.

# The save order of execution

Triggers, as well as declarative tools such as workflows, processes, assignment rules, etc., all form part of what is known as the *save order of execution*. Understanding the save order of execution is key to ensuring that when you write a trigger you use the correct type of trigger and understand how triggers may interact with one another to give unintended behaviors. The save order of execution fires every time that a record is saved against the database - that is an `insert`, `update`, or `upsert` of data. The full save the order of execution is listed below:

1. **Record loaded or initialized**: The original record is loaded from the database if we are updating a record, otherwise we initialize a new record for the system to work with.

2. **Field values loaded and system validation if a standard UI page**: The field values we are setting are loaded into the record and if we are creating the record via the standard UI (whether lightning or classic) then system validation rules are executed. These check:

   • Layout specific rules

   • Required fields populated

   • Field values are in the correct format

   • Field values do not exceed the maximum length

   If coming from another source such as Apex, the system only validates that foreign keys (lookup and master-detail values) are valid.

3. **Before-save flows executed**: In the Spring 20 release, Salesforce introduced before-save flows that allow you to set field values before any triggers run. These flows are executed here.

4. **Before triggers executed**: Any of our triggers in the `before` context are executed and run.

5. **System validation re-run and custom validation run**: Our system validation rules, except layout specific rules, are now re-run after any updates have occurred and our custom validation rules also run to check for incorrect values.

6. **Duplicate rules run**: Any duplicate rules we have enforced are run and if they are specified to block when a duplicate is discovered, the save execution stops, and no further action is taken.

7. **Record saved to the database (not committed)**: At this point, the record is saved to the database and receives an Id. It is not yet committed to the database and may still be rolled back.

8. **After triggers executed**: Any of our triggers in the `after` context are executed and run.

9. **Assignment rules executed**: If we have assignment rules, for example on the Lead object, these are then run.

10. **Auto-response rules executed**: If we have any auto-response rules setup for our Lead or Case object, these are executed.

11. **Workflow rules executed**: Any workflow rules we have defined are now executed.

12. **Update the record again if containing workflow field updates**: If our workflow rule contains field updates, these are run and the record is updated.

13. **If the record has been updated, run** before **and** after **update triggers once more and standard validation**: If as part of our workflow rule execution, the record under save was updated, then the before and after update triggers both fire again once, and only once, more. Additionally, standard validations only are run.

14. **Processes and flows run**: Any processes and flows are run that are fired by either a process or through workflow trigger actions. If any of these save records they then go through the save order of execution.

15. **Escalation rules executed**: Any escalation rules for Case records are executed.

16. **Entitlement rules executed**: Any entitlement rules are run for Case records.

17. **Roll-up summary and cross-object workflow run. If a parent record gets updated it goes through save the order of execution**: If the record contains a field that is used in a roll-up summary or is part of a cross-object workflow rule, then these calculations are performed and the parent record is updated. The parent record then goes through the save order of execution.

18. **If the parent record is changed and a grandparent record contains roll-up summary fields or is in a cross-object workflow, grandparent record gets updated and goes through save procedure**: Just like the previous step, if the parent record is part of a cross-object workflow or roll-up summary then calculations are performed and the grandparent record is updated and undergoes the save order of execution.

19. **Criteria based sharing rules run**: Any sharing of the original record using criteria-based sharing rules is performed and sharing records created.

20. **All records committed to the database**: All changes are then committed to the database.

21. **Post-commit logic is executed**: Any post-commit logic is then executed and run. This includes actions such as sending emails.

As we can see the save order of execution contains a lot of steps and potential updates for our system. Because of this, we want to be careful when we are working with updates and changes to records as this can severely slow down our solution. Now that we have an understanding of the save order of execution and where triggers fit within it, let us now look at how and when we should use each type of trigger.

# When to use each trigger type

As discussed previously, we have a number of different types of triggers that can run. In this section, I want to walk through each type of trigger and when you should look to use it.

## Before insert

`Before insert` triggers are the first trigger that can run on any record and do so before a record has been assigned an `Id` by being saved to the database. We should use `before insert` triggers to set any values on records we are inserting that are based on complex logic, or if we want to run any complex system validation.

We want to set any values here as they will then be set on the record when it is inserted into the database, rather than requiring us to update the record again, stopping the record from having to undergo the save order of execution steps defined above.

For validation before insertion, it is best placed in a `before insert` trigger as if the record fails validation we can then error early and avoid having to rollback the record. Whilst rollback of the record is automatic, by failing the validation early we can ensure that we minimize the amount of work the system has to do and improve our solution's speed.

## After insert

`After insert` triggers run once the record has been saved to the database and been given an Id. At this point, we can query for the record from the database within our transaction context only. If the `after insert` trigger queries for a record using its Id, it will be retrieved, however, if any other transaction were to try and query for the record it would not be available until it is committed to the database at the end of the save order of execution.

We should use `after insert` triggers when we either require the Id, need to query for some other calculated field value, or want to create or update additional records. We may require the `Id` when creating a series of default child records for example, or in passing the record `Id` to an asynchronous process. An example might be that on the insertion of a new account, we may make a call out to a web service that retrieves the account's credit score. We would do this asynchronously, passing the account's

`Id` to the background process to retrieve the data it needed at runtime.

# Before update

A `before update` trigger runs before any changes made to an existing record are saved to the database. We should again use this before trigger for making any additional updates to values on the record or for custom validation logic. In this trigger, as we shall see later, we have access to both the old and new values on the record that enable us to compare the values and then make or validate changes as appropriate. For example, we may wish to validate that a record has changed from one status to another and not skipped an intermediary step. Again, we want to do this in the `before` trigger to fail early.

# After update

An `after update` trigger fires once updates have been written to the database and should be used for either updating or creating related records, or when a value from the save is required, for example, a query to retrieve a formula field. A common use case for `after update` triggers are in calculating a total value for a parent record that is in a lookup relationship. For example, we may have a series of task records related to a contact, and wish to calculate the total number of open tasks related to each contact. For this, we would use an `after update` trigger to retrieve and count all the open tasks in the various states.

# Before delete

The `before delete` trigger runs before a record is deleted from the database and should be used to validate that a record should be deleted and block that deletion otherwise.

# After delete

Once a record deletion has been saved to the database but not committed, the `after delete` trigger runs. This trigger type should be used for cleaning up related records where a cascade delete will not occur, namely when the record being deleted is the parent in a lookup relationship which has not got the *Don't allow deletion of the lookup record that's part of a lookup relationship* option selected. Similarly, we may also use this trigger for updating related records like in our task total example in the `after update` trigger. If we deleted a task, we would want to update the related contact's total.

# After undelete

If a deleted record is retrieved from the recycle bin after it has been re-saved to the database the `after undelete` trigger will fire. This trigger allows us to recreate any relationships or set any values we wish on related records. Again, looking back to our example of tasks related to contacts, if a task was undeleted we would want to update the total number of tasks related to the contact record.

We can see that triggers allow us to implement logic that manipulates and manages our record data throughout the entire record's lifecycle. Within our triggers, we have access to special context variables that enable us to work with the data in various states as well as manage the flow of our trigger.

# Trigger context variables

Within each trigger, we get access to different context variables that enable us to work with the data being changed as well as control the flow of our trigger itself. Let's look at the trigger context variables Salesforce provides in detail:

- `Trigger.isExecuting`: `Trigger.isExecuting` returns a `Boolean` value indicating whether or not the code is running within a trigger context or not. This is a commonly used method when we extract common code from a trigger into an Apex class and wish to undertake different behavior when running within a trigger context.

- `Trigger.isInsert`: `Trigger.isInsert` will return a value of `true` if the current trigger context is an `insert` trigger - that is a new record has been created and is being saved.

- `Trigger.isUpdate`: `Trigger.isUpdate` will return a value of `true` if the current trigger context is an `update` trigger - that is an existing record has been changed and is being saved.

- `Trigger.isDelete`: `Trigger.isDelete` will return a value of `true` if the current trigger context is a `delete` trigger - that is an existing record is being removed from the database.

- `Trigger.isUndelete`: `Trigger.isUndelete` will return a value of `true` if the current trigger context is an `undelete` trigger - that is a record from the recycle bin is being reinstated on the database.

- `Trigger.isBefore`: `Trigger.isBefore` will return a value of `true` if the current trigger is running in the `before` context, i.e. before a record or change has been saved to the database.

- `Trigger.isAfter`: `Trigger.isAfter` will return a value of `true` if the current trigger is running in the `after` context, i.e. after a record or change has been saved to the database.

- `Trigger.new`: `Trigger.new` returns a list of the new versions of the records undergoing the save process which has datatype `List<sObject>`. Records within the `Trigger.new` list are only writeable in the `before` trigger context and any changes made to these records will be saved to the database. Additionally, the `Trigger.new` list is only available in the `insert`, `update` and undelete triggers, in a `delete` trigger, there are no new records.

- `Trigger.newMap`: `Trigger.newMap` returns a map of type `Map<Id, sObject>` where the `Id` keys are the record Ids and the sObjects their corresponding new record versions. The list generated by `Trigger.newMap.values()` is the same list of records available in `Trigger.new`.

- `Trigger.old`: `Trigger.old` is similar to `Trigger.new` in that it returns a list of records undergoing the save process and have the datatype `List<sObject>`. Instead of returning a list of the new version of these records, it returns the old versions of the records as they existed on the database prior to any changes. It is therefore only available in `update` and `delete` triggers as in the `insert` and `undelete` cases there is no old record.

- `Trigger.oldMap`: Similar to `Trigger.newMap`, `Trigger.oldMap` returns a map of type `Map<Id, sObject>` where the `Id` keys are the record Ids and the sObjects their corresponding old record versions from the database before any save occurred. Again, the list generated by `Trigger.oldMap.values()` is the same list of records available in `Trigger.old`.

- `Trigger.operationType`: `Trigger.operationType` returns an enum that is of type `System.TriggerOperation` and corresponds to the current trigger context. Available enum values are:
  - BEFORE_INSERT
  - AFTER_INSERT
  - BEFORE_UPDATE
  - AFTER_UPDATE
  - BEFORE_DELETE
  - AFTER_DELETE
  - AFTER_UNDELETE

- `Trigger.size`: `Trigger.size` returns the number of records that are within the current trigger's invocation, both old and new.

Now that we have an understanding of what triggers are and what contextual data we have available to us, let us begin by writing our first basic trigger.

# Our first trigger

To create our first trigger log into your Salesforce developer environment and open up the Developer Console. Under the **File** menu, select **New** and **Apex Trigger**. In the window that opens, enter ContactTrigger in the **Name** field and choose **Contact** as the sObject before pressing **Submit**. We will be presented with the following code for our trigger, this is the default trigger created by Salesforce:

```
trigger ContactTrigger on Contact (before insert) {

}
```

As we can see, the standard format for a trigger is as follows:

```
trigger TriggerName on sObject (list of applicable contexts) {

}
```

The list of applicable contexts is a comma-separated list of the contexts in which we want our trigger to run. We want our trigger to run in the before insert context only so we do not need to update our code.

We are going to add in some defaulting for our contact which will populate the **Phone** field with the value in the **Mobile Phone** field if the **Phone** field is blank and the **Mobile Phone** field is populated. If both fields are blank we are going to add an error to the record and stop it from being inserted.

So what are the steps to do this? Firstly we are going to need to loop through the records within our Trigger.new list. If we recall we can loop through a list using a for loop as we discussed in the previous chapter, so let's firstly update our code to do that:

```
trigger ContactTrigger on Contact (before insert) {

for(Contact con : Trigger.new) {

    }

}
```

Here we are defining a for loop over the records in the Trigger.new list which is a list of contact records in this instance, and we are calling the iterator i.e. the contact record we are currently working with, con.

The next step is to check to see if both the **Phone** and **Mobile Phone** fields are blank, if so we will want to add our error to the contact record. To check whether both fields are empty we will need to use an `if` statement as follows:

```
trigger ContactTrigger on Contact (before insert) {

for(Contact con : Trigger.new) {

if(con.Phone == null && con.MobilePhone == null) {

    }

  }

}
```

Here we can recall from *Chapter 5: Control Statements and Operators* that the double ampersand && symbol denotes a logical AND operation, so we are returning `true` in our `if` statement when both the **Phone** field is equal to `null` (empty) and the **Mobile Phone** field is equal to `null`. The next step then is to add an error to the record in the code block to be executed for the `if` statement. Salesforce provides a method on every `sObject` instance called `addError` which takes in a single parameter of an error message. We can now add in the line of code to use that:

```
trigger ContactTrigger on Contact (before insert) {

for(Contact con : Trigger.new) {

if(con.Phone == null && con.MobilePhone == null) {

con.addError('One of either phone or mobile phone must be populated.');

    }

  }

}
```

We have added in the message *One of either phone or mobile phones must be populated* to be displayed should we create a contact meeting these criteria. At this point let us save our trigger by either pressing *Ctrl + S / CMD + S* or going to **File** and choosing **Save**. Once this has saved switch over to the standard user interface and try to create a contact with no value in either the **Phone** or **Mobile Phone** fields and the error should be displayed, as shown in the image below:

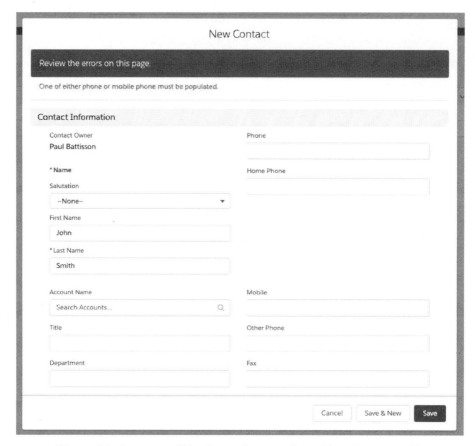

***Figure 6.1:*** *An error will be thrown by our trigger if we do not provide the data needed*

If you populate either of those fields and save again the error should not fire and the record will save.

Congratulations! You have just written, deployed, and run your first Apex trigger and our first full piece of Apex code!

Let's finish off our example by adding in the logic to populate the **Phone** field if it is empty with the value from the **Mobile Phone** field. For this we will want to extend our existing `if` statement to have an `elseif` option as a second branch as shown below. This second if should check that our **Phone** field has the value `null` and that the **Mobile Phone** field is not `null`.

```
trigger ContactTrigger on Contact (before insert) {

for(Contact con : Trigger.new) {

if(con.Phone == null && con.MobilePhone == null) {
```

```
con.addError('One of either phone or mobile phone must be populated.');

    } else if(con.Phone == null && con.MobilePhone != null) {


}

    }

}
```

Finally, if these conditions are met we want to set the value of the **Phone** field to be the value of the **Mobile Phone** field:

```
trigger ContactTrigger on Contact (before insert) {

for(Contact con : Trigger.new) {

if(con.Phone == null && con.MobilePhone == null) {

con.addError('One of either phone or mobile phone must be populated.');

    } else if(con.Phone == null && con.MobilePhone != null) {

con.Phone = con.MobilePhone;

    }

    }

}
```

Again, save the trigger and test it in your user interface. We can see that the trigger runs and correctly populates the **Phone** field with the value of the **Mobile Phone** field when it is empty.

We have now written a trigger that contains a number of the topics we have covered before - a `for` loop, an `if-else` with Boolean logic, assignment of field values, and adding an error to a record. Not a bad start for 9 lines of code! We should now pause to discuss an important topic when it comes to triggers, bulkification.

# Bulkification of triggers

When working with Salesforce triggers, there are a few key considerations we have to be aware of. The first of which is that Salesforce will pass in up to 200 records for processing within the trigger, that is the size of `Trigger.new` can be up to 200 records. This is for instances where multiple records are being created at once, for example via a data load, and means that we must ensure that we write our triggers in a way that handles data efficiently.

# An un-bulkified trigger

Let's consider the following example. We want to have a trigger which when an opportunity is marked as closed won, a set of invoice records are created using a custom invoice object `Invoice__c`. A potential set of code for this trigger is as follows:

```
trigger OpportunityTrigger on Opportunity (after update) {

for(Opportunity opp : Trigger.new) {

if(opp.StageName == 'Closed/Won' &&Trigger.oldMap.get(opp.Id).StageName
!= 'Closed/Won') {


Invoice__c firstInvoice = new Invoice__c();

firstInvoice.Amount__c = opp.Amount * 0.5;

firstInvoice.Opportunity__c = opp.Id;


Invoice__c secondInvoice = new Invoice__c();

secondInvoice.Amount__c = opp.Amount * 0.3;

secondInvoice.Opportunity__c = opp.Id;


Invoice__c thirdInvoice = new Invoice__c();

thirdInvoice.Amount__c = opp.Amount * 0.2;

thirdInvoice.Opportunity__c = opp.Id;


        insert new List<Invoice__c>{firstInvoice, secondInvoice,
        thirdInvoice};
    }
  }
}
```

Here we are creating three related `Invoice__c` records which will have 50%, 30%, and 20% of the total amount respectively to invoice the customer. We are then inserting them before moving on to processing for the next opportunity in the list.

This code will function perfectly fine and if we were to test it within our organization we would find that it ran without any issues. However, what if we were to close 151 opportunities at once as part of a data load or a month-end process for repeat opportunities?

For every opportunity record in our trigger, we are performing a single DML statement. The governor limit for the number of DML statements per transaction is set at 150. This means on the 151st opportunity record we would get a governor limit exception. We may even encounter this limit earlier in fact if we had a trigger on the `Invoice__c` object that was also performing some DML.

This example highlights how we need to always be thinking of bulkification within our trigger code. Bulkification is the term for ensuring that your Apex code will work on multiple records at once in a scalable fashion, rather than a single record at a time.

# Bulkifying our trigger

How would we bulkily this trigger? In this example, it is pretty simple for us to do. We know that we want to reduce the number of DML statements down from one per opportunity on the list. We also know that DML statements can fire on lists of records (we are already doing that) so could we group the invoice records more effectively for insertion? Let's see how we could do this in the code below:

```
trigger OpportunityTrigger on Opportunity (after update) {

    List<Invoice__c> newInvoices = new List<Invoice__c>();

for(Opportunity opp : Trigger.new) {

if(opp.StageName == 'Closed/Won' && Trigger.oldMap.get(opp.Id).StageName
!= 'Closed/Won') {

Invoice__c firstInvoice = new Invoice__c();

firstInvoice.Amount__c = opp.Amount * 0.5;

firstInvoice.Opportunity__c = opp.Id;

newInvoices.add(firstInvoice);
```

```
Invoice__c secondInvoice = new Invoice__c();

secondInvoice.Amount__c = opp.Amount * 0.3;

secondInvoice.Opportunity__c = opp.Id;

newInvoices.add(secondInvoice);


Invoice__c thirdInvoice = new Invoice__c();

thirdInvoice.Amount__c = opp.Amount * 0.2;

thirdInvoice.Opportunity__c = opp.Id;

newInvoices.add(thirdInvoice);

    }

    }


    insert newInvoices;

}
```

In this improved trigger, we have instantiated a new variable `newInvoices` first which has the data type `List<Invoice__c>` and will hold our created invoices. We then loop through as before, but this time we add each newly created invoice to the `newInvoices` list and make one DML statement at the very end, inserting all of the records in our `newInvoices` list. We have now gone from running a DML statement per opportunity to a single DML statement regardless of how many opportunities we update.

# Bulkification for success

As we have seen, bulkification is a key consideration whenever we are writing trigger code. Not only will it help us avoid governor limits as we have seen above, but it will also improve the speed of our code overall. In our original trigger, when we ran the DML statement per record under save, we would then invoke the save order of execution multiple times for the new invoice records. If we have triggers, workflow, processes, and other actions all firing in the save order of execution for the invoice records, this will slow down the overall running time for the trigger. If instead we make a single DML statement and have bulkified the items that are then processing the invoice records, our solution will be much faster overall.

# Conclusion

In this chapter, we have gone through what an Apex trigger is, how they operate, and where they are used within the system. We have seen how we can define a trigger and execute it in different contexts. We have discussed what these contexts are and the different variables available for those contexts to use to make working with records simpler. Finally, we took an existing trigger and looked at how and why we should bulkily it in order to ensure that it operates in a manner that is both efficient for performance, but also in how utilizes our governor limits to avoid exceptions.

# Questions

1.  What are the different types of triggers?
2.  What is different about a record in an after insert trigger compared to in the before insert trigger?
3.  What does it mean to bulkify a trigger?
4.  Why is bulkification important?

# CHAPTER 7
# SOQL

## Structure

In this chapter we will cover:

- What is SOQL?
- How SOQL differs from SQL
- The structure of a SOQL statement
- How to filter queries
- How to use aggregate functions
- How to work with relationships in SOQL

## Objectives

By the end of this chapter you should:

- Know how to write SOQL queries that work on multiple related records
- Know how to filter the results returned in a SOQL query
- How to use aggregate functions
- The differences between SOQL and SQL

So far we have learned how to create records in memory, assign them to variables, set values for their fields, and then insert them into the Salesforce database. In this chapter, we are going to look at how we can retrieve data from the Salesforce database so we can manipulate and update it using Apex.

# What is SOQL?

**SOQL** stands for **S**alesforce **O**bject **Q**uery **L**anguage and is the querying language provided by Salesforce to enable us to query and retrieve data from the Salesforce database. It is analogous to SQL used within other databases, with a few differences due to the way in which the Salesforce database is structured.

Firstly, within SOQL there are no DML operations. As we have seen in *Chapter 3: Variables in Apex*, DML in Apex is performed through the use of DML statements on records or collections of records and is not performed through the query syntax as in other SQL variants. For this reason, you may see documentation referring to SOQL as being equivalent to the SQL SELECT statement.

Secondly, as with all code on the Salesforce platform, SOQL is bound by governor limits. Developers are limited to making 100 queries within a single transaction and returning across these queries a maximum of 50,000 rows of data. This means that when we are working with a set of SOQL queries we should take care to bulkify our queries and only retrieve the data needed.

# The Force.com Query Optimizer

Another key difference between SOQL and SQL is that SOQL is not run itself against the database but passes through the Force.com Query Optimizer upon execution. The optimizer is responsible for taking a SOQL query and determining the correct and optimal SQL syntax to run against the underlying database. The optimizer runs a multi-step process as shown in the diagram below:

*Figure 7.1: The Force.com Query Optimizer*

Firstly, the optimizer reviews a set of pre-calculated statistics to determine which table to run the query against and which filters in the query are most selective to enable the query to be as efficient as possible. These statistics are calculated weekly and enable the system to use a combination of the user's visibility (i.e. which records the user running the query can see due to sharing) and the filter selectivity, to then proceed to build a SQL query. This SQL query is produced by the optimizer to run against the database tables that make up the underlying infrastructure of the Salesforce platform. Once this query has been created, it is executed, and the results are then parsed and returned to the user.

# SOQL statement structure

For any developer familiar with ANSI SQL, SOQL will follow a very familiar structure. A SOQL query in its most basic form has the following format:

```
SELECT    fieldList    FROM    sObject    {WHERE    filterConditions}{LIMIT
maxRowsToRetrieve}
```

Here fieldList is a comma-separated list of field API names and sObject is the sObject API name. Both the WHERE and LIMIT clauses are optional here, however, it is a best practice to always include at least one. In the WHERE clause, filterConditions is an expression to filter the records (for example retrieving records where a field has a particular value) and the maxRowsToRetrieve parameter in the LIMIT clause is an integer to limit the number of rows of data returned. Other clauses are available, which we will discuss later in the chapter, but the above syntax is the most common and basic structure for any SOQL query.

Switching to our Developer Console, at the bottom of the window we can see there is a tab labeled **Query Editor** as shown below. This tab enables us to run a query against the database and see the results in a tabular format for us to view the data returned by the query. It is an extremely useful tool during development to enable us to write and validate our queries:

*Figure 7.2: The Query Editor*

If you open this tab and enter the following code into the panel with the **Enter SOQL or SOSL..** placeholder text:

```
SELECT Id, Name FROM Account LIMIT 10
```

Comparing this query against our syntax above we can see that:

- We are retrieving the `Id` and `Name` fields.
- They are from the account `sObject` so we will be retrieving account records.
- We are only going to retrieve the first 10 records the database finds.

If we press the **Execute** button at the bottom of the screen, the query will be executed against the database and we can see that a table is displayed in the main panel showing 10 account records, their Ids, and Names. Your screen should look like the image below (note the returned records may differ):

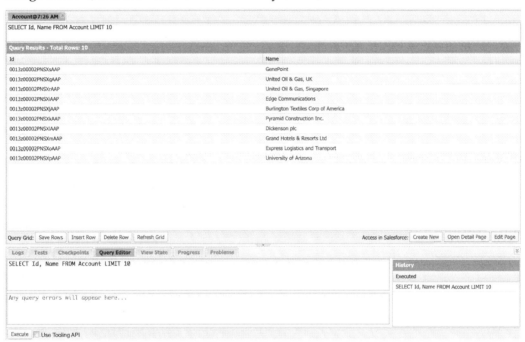

***Figure 7.3:*** *Viewing a query's results in the Developer Console*

We have now executed our first SOQL query against the database and retrieved a limited set of data from the object. It is more common however to filter the results we wish to get using field values and expressions. Let's say we had a requirement to only retrieve the Ids and Names of those accounts with annual revenue over $100,000,000. How would we update the SOQL query to do so?

Firstly, we need to determine what field or fields we will be filtering on to define our filter logic. In this case, we will be using the `AnnualRevenue` field only. We know from *Chapter 5: Control Statements and Operators* that we can use the > operator to compare a value, and we have the value we want to be greater than. So our WHERE clause would be:

```
WHERE AnnualRevenue > 100000000
```

We can now remove the LIMIT clause as well as we want to retrieve all the matching accounts, and so our updated query becomes:

```
SELECT Id, Name, AnnualRevenue FROM Account WHERE AnnualRevenue > 100000000
```

If we execute that in our query editor, we get a new tab in the Developer Console with the matching rows returned as shown below:

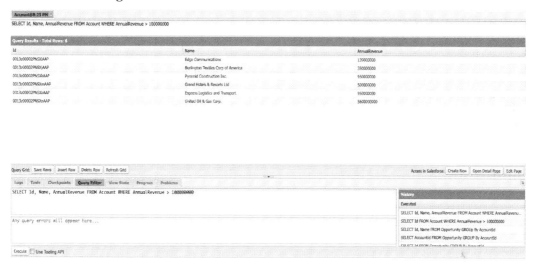

*Figure 7.4: Results from our filtered query*

# Executing SOQL in Apex

We have seen how to execute SOQL within the query editor, however, we want to execute the query within our Apex code to retrieve records from the database for us to work with.

As had been briefly hinted at in *Chapter 5: Control Statements and Operators*, when we execute a SOQL query in Apex we receive a list of that object's type back for us to work with. In the previous example, the data returned would have type List<Account>. Again it is worth pausing a moment here to note that this is a key difference between Salesforce and other platforms.

If we were working with a combination of say C# and MS SQL Server, or Java and Oracle, we would have to define classes for the data types to be marshaled into for us to work with them. This is typically done using an **Object-Relational Mapping**

**(ORM)** tool. This tool enables the programming language to work with the data in a structured format so that the developer can access and create records in a simpler fashion. Salesforce knows that Apex is only run on their platform and against their database, and so have abstracted away from any need for an ORM enabling developers to work with sObjects in Apex far more readily.

As an example, if we wanted to retrieve all of these accounts with annual revenue over $100,000,000 and then sum up their annual revenue to get a total, we could do this by looping through the list of records that are retrieved from our query above as shown in the code block below:

```
List<Account> accs = [SELECT Id, Name, AnnualRevenue FROM Account WHERE
AnnualRevenue > 100000000];

Decimal total = 0;

for(Account acc : accs) {

total += acc.AnnualRevenue;

}
```

There are a few ways we can improve this code to make it more performant and cleaner. Firstly, the only field we are accessing from the account records in our loop is the `AnnualRevenue` field. It is a best practice to ensure that you only query and retrieve the required fields from the database.

It should also be noted that the `Id` field is always returned for a record regardless, so there is no need to define it in the query. Whether you wish to include the `Id` field or not is therefore down to your preference in terms of clarity. I have worked with teams where it was always explicitly defined and in teams where it was always excluded. My habit is to include the `Id` explicitly in the query only if I am going to reference the `Id` field throughout the code or in the where clause. In this case, we are not so I would not list the `Id` field:

This would update our code to

```
List<Account> accs = [SELECT AnnualRevenue FROM Account WHERE AnnualRevenue
> 100000000];

Decimal total = 0;

for(Account acc : accs) {

total += acc.AnnualRevenue;

}
```

Our query here is cleaner to read and is not bringing back any data we do not require.

We can improve this code further still by noting that we are not using the `accs` variable anywhere else except for in the loop and so we are holding additional data in memory that will not be needed. As such we can remove the `accs` variable and simply place our query into the `for` loop initialization for the records to be accessed.

```
Decimal total = 0;

for(Account acc : [SELECT AnnualRevenue FROM Account WHERE AnnualRevenue
> 100000000]) {

total += acc.AnnualRevenue;

}
```

This looks much cleaner, keeps us from storing additional data in memory, and allows us to keep the code easier to read and review inline.

# Using binding variables

Typically, we will want our queries to use a value from elsewhere within our Apex code in a dynamic way for filtering. For example, when we previously discussed wanting to count the number of open tasks related to a specific contact, we would need to use the `Id` for the contact record as part of our query. This value would only be known at runtime and stored in some variable we were working with, so we would want to use the value within that variable. The way of doing this is through what is known as a *bind variable* or through the process of binding variables.

Taking our example of retrieving open tasks related to a contact, let's again analyze what we would need to do to build up our query. Firstly, what fields do we need to retrieve? If we are counting, only the `Id` field is needed as at least 1 field must be specified within the `SELECT` statement. For filtering, we want to check that the `IsClosed` field on the `Task` is equal to false. Finally, we want to check that the value in the `WhoId` field on the task is the `Id` for our contact. The code for this would be as follows:

```
Contact con; //We have a variable con which is set to the Contact we are
wanting to retrieve tasks for

List<Task> tasks = [SELECT Id FROM Task WHERE IsClosed = false AND WhoId
= :con.Id];
```

We can see that we have used a logical `AND` here to specify that we wish both of our filter criteria to be met. We can combine filters using `AND`, `OR`, and `NOT` to create complex filter criteria as needed. We can also see that we have referenced the `Id` from our `con` variable as `:con.Id`. The colon `:` mark here preceding the variable name marks this as a bind variable to be evaluated at run time and the value be inserted into the query.

We can also bind to variables that are lists or sets and us a special keyword `IN`. For example, if instead of retrieving the tasks for only a single contact we wanted to retrieve the tasks for multiple contacts, we could group the respective ids for the contacts into a set and then query for task records where the `WhoId` is in the set. We can see this below:

```
//We have a variable conIds which are of type Set<Id> and is the Ids of
all contacts we are retrieving related tasks for
```

```
List<Task> tasks = [SELECT Id FROM Task WHERE IsClosed = false AND WhoId
IN :conIds];
```

This provides us with a nice way of working to bulkify our queries in the future. Instead of making multiple queries, one for each separate contact, we should create a set of all the contact Ids, and then perform a single query to process the results. We want to use a set as it will ensure that we have no duplicate Ids passed into the query keeping it efficient.

# Aggregate functions and grouping

We could improve upon this example query even further however, by using grouping and aggregate functions. These features of SOQL are used together to automate the gathering of statistics related to records and have them grouped for use in a way that can save writing further Apex code to process the data.

## Aggregate functions

Aggregate functions are numeric functions that run on a particular field to return a statistic about the values of that field in a given set of records that meet some query criteria. In this section we will briefly cover what the functions are and how they are used:

- `COUNT()` and `COUNT(field)`: `COUNT()` is possibly the most commonly used of the aggregate functions and returns the number of records meeting the defined filter criteria. If we are also grouping for a particular field, we should use `COUNT(field)` where the `field` is the field we are also grouping by. Note that `COUNT(Id)` does not require a grouping and is equivalent to the `COUNT(*)` syntax found in ANSI SQL.

- `COUNT_DISTINCT(field)`: `COUNT_DISTINCT` takes a field and performs a count where records with `null` values on the field are excluded.

- `AVG(numeric_field)`: The `AVG` function takes in a numerical field and returns an average value for the field across all records matching the criteria.

- `MIN(numeric_field)` and `MAX(numeric_field)`: The `MIN` and `MAX` functions take a specified field name and then return respectively the minimum or maximum value of that field in records meeting the query filter criteria.

- `SUM(numeric_field)`: The `SUM` function totals the values of a numeric field across all records matching the query filter criteria.

Let's look at some examples. If we wanted to count the number of unique accounts we had we could query:

```
SELECT COUNT(Id) FROM Account
```

If we wanted to get the average annual revenue for our accounts it would be

```
SELECT AVG(AnnualRevenue) FROM Account
```

When working with aggregate functions, the return type of our query changes from being `List<sObject>` to `List<AggregateResult>`. The `AggregateResult` type is a special type only available when working with aggregate functions and behaves like a map with a key of type `String`. By default, the aggregate function we call in the query is stored on the aggregate result as `exprX` where `X` is the order of the field starting at 0. For example:

```
List<AggregateResult> results = [SELECT COUNT(Id), AVG(AnnualRevenue)
FROM Account];

//We know we will only retrieve a single row here as we are not grouping
as we will see shortly

System.debug('Number of records = ' + results[0].get('expr0'));

System.debug('Average Annual Revenue = ' + results[0].get('expr1'));
```

As noted in this block, we will see how grouping will return multiple rows here, but because we have no grouping we can be confident in accessing the first record in the list using the array index notation `results[0]`. We can then see how the first aggregate function we call, `COUNT(Id)` is returned by calling `get('expr0')` and the second function, `AVG(AnnualRevenue)` is retrieved by calling `get('expr1')`.

Because this is not the easiest code to read, we can add aliases to these as shown below that provide a more human readable naming scheme:

```
List<AggregateResult> results = [SELECT COUNT(Id) number, AVG(AnnualRevenue)
average FROM Account];

System.debug('Number of records = ' + results[0].get('number'));

System.debug('Average Annual Revenue = ' + results[0].get('average'));
```

# Grouping

We can use grouping in combination with our aggregate functions to enable us to make the statistics we are gathering more granular for our records. To add a grouping, we append GROUP BY fieldName to the end of our query and it will bundle our aggregate results based upon the fieldName specified. Going back to our example with tasks associated to contacts, we could take our previous query:

```
//We have a variable conIds which is of type Set<Id> and is the Ids of all
contacts we are retrieving related tasks for

List<Task> tasks = [SELECT Id FROM Task WHERE IsClosed = false AND WhoId
IN :conIds];
```

And update it to use aggregate functions and a grouping clause to give us the totals we are looking for:

```
//We have a variable conIds which is of type Set<Id> and is the Ids of all
contacts we are retrieving related tasks for

List<AggregateResult> results = [SELECT WhoId, COUNT(Id) number FROM Task
WHERE IsClosed = false AND WhoId IN :conIds GROUP BY WhoId];

for(AggregateResult res : results) {

System.debug('For the contact with Id ' + res.get('WhoId') + ' we have '
+ res.get('number') + ' of open tasks');

}
```

Our updated query uses the same WHERE clause filters and binding variables to filter the results down to the required set. Our aggregate function returns for us the statistic we are interested in and we have included the WhoId field in our SELECT statement to allow us to display the Id of the related contact. We have also added a grouping using the GROUP BY clause and have told the query to group by the WhoId for the tasks. We are then looping through the results we retrieve and printing out the details for us to see in the debug log. Note that because we are grouping by WhoId and listing it in fields for the SELECT statement we can then retrieve that from the aggregate result using get('WhoId').

# An updated trigger example

Let us now bring a few of these concepts together in an updated trigger example. We are going to define a trigger for the task object which will increment the number of open tasks for a contact every time a new one is added and recalculate the number of open tasks associated with a contact every time that a task is closed. For this, we will use a combination of our flow statements, queries, and DML to make the necessary changes.

Firstly, log into your developer environment and on the Contact object add a new number field called *No of Open Tasks* with an API name No_of_Open_Tasks__c. This is the field we are going to populate in our trigger and you can see the definition screen in my environment below.

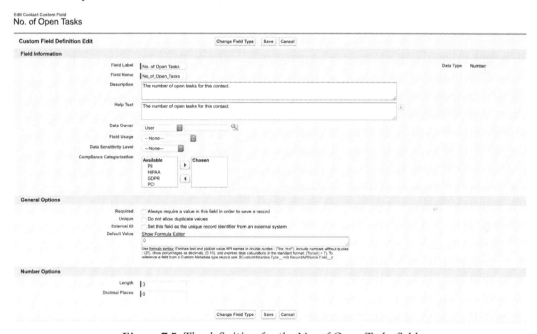

***Figure 7.5:*** *The definition for the No. of Open Tasks field*

Now back in the Developer Console, define a new trigger called TaskTrigger on the Task object and update it to run on both after insert and after update:

```
trigger TaskTrigger on Task (after insert, after update) {


}
```

We have added the `after insert` context here to ensure that we are updating the total field every time a new task is added. We should separate our code by checking to see whether we are in an insert or update operation. To do that, let's use a switch statement on the `Trigger.operationType` context variable.

```
trigger TaskTrigger on Task (after insert, after update) {

    switch on Trigger.operationType {

        when AFTER_INSERT {


        }

        when AFTER_UPDATE {


        }

    }

}
```

For our `after insert` code, we want to loop through all the new tasks, retrieve the related contact, and increment the `No_of_Open_Tasks__c` field by 1 for each task for that contact. The first step is retrieving a list of contact Ids. The relevant `Id` would be stored in the `WhoId` field, however, this is a polymorphic field - that is it can contain an `Id` for either a contact or a lead. We should, therefore, check that it is for contact by validating that the `Id` has the correct `sObject` prefix.

Each `sObject` in Salesforce has a special prefix of 3 characters for the object, for example, the one for an account is 001 and for contact is 003. We will need to validate that the `Id` in the `WhoId` field starts with 003[1]. Our code to do this first step then, looping through the new tasks and gathering the ids would look as follows, firstly define a new set of Ids (we don't want duplicates) to hold our contact Ids:

```
Set<Id> contactIds = new Set<Id>();
```

Then loop through the list of new tasks in our `Trigger.new` context variable:

```
Set<Id> contactIds = new Set<Id>();

for(Task t : Trigger.new) {
```

---

1   If we were working with a custom object we would retrieve this prefix using a schema query, however it is fixed for standard objects so we can hardcode for this example.

```
}
```

For each task t, we need to check that:

- The WhoId is not null
- The WhoId starts with 003

If both these conditions are met add it to the set. We can check the second requirement using the startsWith() method available to strings, however we will first need to convert our Id to a string using String.valueOf(). We can see this all together in the code below:

```
Set<Id> contactIds = new Set<Id>();

for(Task t : Trigger.new) {

if(t.WhoId != null && String.valueOf(t.WhoId).startsWith('003')) {

contactIds.add(t.WhoId);

}

}
```

Note that the String.valueOf method returns a String instance and the startsWith method is available on String instances. We can therefore chain our methods as we have above to make our code more concise. If it is not entirely clear what this code is doing, we could rewrite as:

```
Set<Id>contactIds = new Set<Id>();

for(Task t : Trigger.new) {

    String whoString = String.valueOf(t.WhoId);

if(t.WhoId != null &&whoString.startsWith('003')) {

contactIds.add(t.WhoId);

    }

}
```

Both sets of code are equivalent. We will use the more concise first version throughout the rest of the chapter.

Now that we have the set of Ids for the relevant contact records, we can query for them from the database. We will need to retrieve the No_of_Open_Tasks__c field to update:

```
Set<Id> contactIds = new Set<Id>();

for(Task t : Trigger.new) {

if(t.WhoId != null && String.valueOf(t.WhoId).startsWith('003')) {

contactIds.add(t.WhoId);

}

}
```

```
List<Contact> contacts = [SELECT Id, No_of_Open_Tasks__c FROM Contact
WHERE Id in :contactIds];
```

At this point, it would be tempting to simply loop through these contact records, increment the No_of_Open_Tasks__c field by one and update the records. However, this may mean we are missing an edge case - what would happen if we were inserting multiple new tasks for the same contact in this transaction? Our code would not be updating the values correctly so we need to rethink. In this case, we want to loop through the tasks and update the matching contact record as many times as is relevant before updating. We therefore need a way of collecting together our contacts so that we can retrieve a contact from the collection using the record Id. This is a perfect use case for a map and also allows us to learn about a handy feature Salesforce provide.

When we have a list of sObjects, Salesforce has a way of creating a map directly from this list of type Map<Id, sObject>. For each record in the list we have an entry in the map where the key is the record Id and the value is the record instance. You can either use a list of sObjects such as our contacts variable above, or use a SOQL query. If we update our code to use this we would then have the following:

```
Set<Id> contactIds = new Set<Id>();

for(Task t : Trigger.new) {

if(t.WhoId != null && String.valueOf(t.WhoId).startsWith('003')) {

contactIds.add(t.WhoId);

}

}
```

```
Map<Id, Contact> contactMap = new Map<Id, Contact>([SELECT Id, No_of_
Open_Tasks__c FROM Contact WHERE Id in :contactIds]);
```

We can see the way of instantiating this map is to simply pass in the list or query to the constructor (the correct name for the parentheses) and Salesforce will do the rest for us. Now we can loop through our tasks again and if the contactMap contains the WhoId value, we retrieve the record and increment the No_of_Open_Tasks__c:

```
Set<Id> contactIds = new Set<Id>();

for(Task t : Trigger.new) {

if(t.WhoId != null && String.valueOf(t.WhoId).startsWith('003')) {

contactIds.add(t.WhoId);

}

    }
```

```
Map<Id, Contact> contactMap = new Map<Id, Contact>([SELECT Id, No_of_
Open_Tasks__c FROM Contact WHERE Id in :contactIds]);


for(Task t : Trigger.new) {

if(contactMap.containsKey(t.WhoId)) {

contactMap.get(t.WhoId).No_of_Open_Tasks__c += 1;

}

}
```

The statement contactMap.get(t.WhoId).No_of_Open_Tasks__c += 1; had a number of things happening that are worth stepping through individually. The first part contactMap.get(t.WhoId) retrieves the contact record from our map. If we wanted we could have defined a variable with a type of Contact to hold the data, but we are not using it elsewhere in our code so is better kept inline. We then access the No_of_Open_Tasks__c field on that record by calling .No_of_Open_Tasks__c on the contact instance retrieved, and increment it by calling += 1. This is another example of using method chaining to make the code more concise and easier to read.

Finally we can then call the update DML statement on the list of contacts to update the records. We retrieve this list from our map using the .values() method:

```
Set<Id> contactIds = new Set<Id>();

for(Task t : Trigger.new) {

if(t.WhoId != null && String.valueOf(t.WhoId).startsWith('003')) {

contactIds.add(t.WhoId);

}


                                                                    }



Map<Id, Contact> contactMap = new Map<Id, Contact>([SELECT Id, No_of_
Open_Tasks__c FROM Contact WHERE Id in :contactIds]);


for(Task t : Trigger.new) {

if(contactMap.containsKey(t.WhoId)) {

contactMap.get(t.WhoId).No_of_Open_Tasks__c += 1;

}


                                                                    }



update contactMap.values();
```

Our trigger should now look as follows:

```
trigger TaskTrigger on Task (after insert, after update) {

    switch on Trigger.operationType {

        when AFTER_INSERT {

            Set<Id> contactIds = new Set<Id>();

for(Task t : Trigger.new) {

if(t.WhoId != null && String.valueOf(t.WhoId).startsWith('003')) {

contactIds.add(t.WhoId);

            }

                }
```

```
Map<Id, Contact> contactMap = new Map<Id, Contact>([SELECT Id, No_of_
Open_Tasks__c FROM Contact WHERE Id in :contactIds]);


for(Task t : Trigger.new) {

if(contactMap.containsKey(t.WhoId)) {

contactMap.get(t.WhoId).No_of_Open_Tasks__c += 1;

        }

          }


      update contactMap.values();

    }

    when AFTER_UPDATE {


    }

  }

}
```

Next we need to deal with our after update logic. Here we again want to start by looping through all the new tasks and checking that the IsClosed field is true on the new instance of the record and false on the old instance. To do this we will be comparing the value of the record in Trigger.new and the record we retrieve from Trigger.oldMap. We will again need to check that the WhoId is not null and that we have the Id for a contact record. If we meet all these criteria then we want to add the contact Id for processing:

```
Set<Id> contactIds = new Set<Id>();

for(Task t : Trigger.new) {

if(t.IsClosed && !Trigger.oldMap.get(t.Id).IsClosed && t.WhoId != null &&
String.valueOf(t.WhoId).startsWith('003')) {

contactIds.add(t.WhoId);
```

```
}

}
```

Our if statement contains 4 criteria we are using together. Firstly, checking IsClosed is true on the new record instance. Checkbox fields have a Boolean datatype in Apex so we do not need to do a comparison and can simply use the value directly.

Next we check the value of IsClosed on the corresponding previous instance of the record is not true. We run Trigger.oldMap.get(t.Id) to retrieve the previous Task record, then access the IsClosed field using the dot notation. As we want IsClosed to be false, for our AND logic to work we use the NOT or inverse operator ! to get the inverted value. So if our IsClosed checkbox is unchecked, i.e. false, the !operator will invert this to true.

Finally we repeat the same logic as in our insert code path to check WhoId is not null and is the Id for a Contact record. As we need all 4 of these items to be true we combine them logically using multiple AND && operators.

We are now presented with an option. We could choose to query all of the contacts within our selected set, loop through the records in a manner similar to how we did before, and then decrement the No_of_Open_Tasks__c field as needed. Instead, we are going to use 2 queries, the first our query for the contact records into a map for usage, and the second an aggregate query on the task object where we group by the WhoId to get totals. There is little difference between these two choices, so we will work with the aggregate query to see how we can use one in a real scenario. For this, we will also need to set all the values to 0 first (to deal with the situation where we have no open tasks for the aggregate query to return).

Firstly, as before, we query for all of our contacts and place them into a map:

```
Set<Id> contactIds = new Set<Id>();

for(Task t : Trigger.new) {

if(t.IsClosed && !Trigger.oldMap.get(t.Id).IsClosed && t.WhoId != null &&
String.valueOf(t.WhoId).startsWith('003')) {

contactIds.add(t.WhoId);

}

        }
```

```
Map<Id, Contact> contactMap = new Map<Id, Contact>([SELECT Id, No_of_
Open_Tasks__c FROM Contact WHERE Id in :contactIds]);
```

As mentioned, we must now loop through all these contacts and set the No_of_Open_ Tasks__c for us to then correctly set the value from our aggregate query if a value is returned:

```
Set<Id> contactIds = new Set<Id>();

for(Task t : Trigger.new) {

if(t.IsClosed && !Trigger.oldMap.get(t.Id).IsClosed && t.WhoId != null &&
String.valueOf(t.WhoId).startsWith('003')) {

contactIds.add(t.WhoId);

}

        }
```

```
Map<Id, Contact> contactMap = new Map<Id, Contact>([SELECT Id, No_of_
Open_Tasks__c FROM Contact WHERE Id in :contactIds]);


for(Contact con : contactMap.values()) {

con.No_of_Open_Tasks__c = 0;

}
```

We are then going to run our aggregate query and loop through the results immediately, we do not need to store the query results in a variable for use:

```
Set<Id> contactIds = new Set<Id>();

for(Task t : Trigger.new) {

if(t.IsClosed && !Trigger.oldMap.get(t.Id).IsClosed && t.WhoId != null &&
String.valueOf(t.WhoId).startsWith('003')) {

contactIds.add(t.WhoId);

}

                                                                }
```

```
Map<Id, Contact> contactMap = new Map<Id, Contact>([SELECT Id, No_of_
Open_Tasks__c FROM Contact WHERE Id in :contactIds]);


for(Contact con : contactMap.values()) {

con.No_of_Open_Tasks__c = 0;

                                                                    }



for(AggregateResult ar : [SELECT WhoId, COUNT(Id) total FROM Task WHERE
IsClosed = false AND WhoId in :contactIds GROUP BY WhoId]) {


}
```

We are then going to retrieve the correct contact from our `contactMap` using the `WhoId` on the ar instance variable and set the `No_of_Open_Tasks__c` to be the total:

```
Set<Td> contactIds = new Set<Id>();

for(Task t : Trigger.new) {

if(t.IsClosed && !Trigger.oldMap.get(t.Id).IsClosed && t.WhoId != null &&
String.valueOf(t.WhoId).startsWith('003')) {

contactIds.add(t.WhoId);

}

                                                                    }



Map<Id, Contact> contactMap = new Map<Id, Contact>([SELECT Id, No_of_
Open_Tasks__c FROM Contact WHERE Id in :contactIds]);


for(Contact con : contactMap.values()) {

con.No_of_Open_Tasks__c = 0;

                                                                    }
```

```
for(AggregateResult ar : [SELECT WhoId, COUNT(Id) total FROM Task WHERE
IsClosed = false AND WhoId in :contactIds GROUP BY WhoId]) {

String who = String.valueOf(ar.get('WhoId'));

Decimal total = (Decimal)(ar.get('total'));

contactMap.get(who).No_of_Open_Tasks__c = total;

}
```

Because we have to cast the values from our AggregateResult to the correct type, I have separated the casting and setting of the value for No_of_Open_Tasks__c onto 3 lines for improved readability. This could all have been done on a single line as:

```
contactMap.get(String.valueOf(ar.get('WhoId'))).No_of_Open_Tasks__c   =
(Decimal)(ar.get('total'));
```

I am sure you will agree that the 3 line version is more readable and so we have separated for us to work with.

Finally we call our update DML statement on the list of contacts in the map. Our final trigger version will look like:

```
trigger TaskTrigger on Task (after insert, after update) {

    switch on Trigger.operationType {

        when AFTER_INSERT {

            Set<Id> contactIds = new Set<Id>();

for(Task t : Trigger.new) {

if(t.WhoId != null && String.valueOf(t.WhoId).startsWith('003')) {

contactIds.add(t.WhoId);

            }

                }


            Map<Id, Contact> contactMap = new Map<Id, Contact>([SELECT Id,
            No_of_Open_Tasks__c FROM Contact WHERE Id in :contactIds]);


for(Task t : Trigger.new) {
```

```
if(contactMap.containsKey(t.WhoId)) {

contactMap.get(t.WhoId).No_of_Open_Tasks__c += 1;

        }

        }


        update contactMap.values();

    }

    when AFTER_UPDATE {

        Set<Id> contactIds = new Set<Id>();

for(Task t : Trigger.new) {

if(t.IsClosed && !Trigger.oldMap.get(t.Id).IsClosed && t.WhoId != null &&
String.valueOf(t.WhoId).startsWith('003')) {

contactIds.add(t.WhoId);

        }

            }


        Map<Id, Contact> contactMap = new Map<Id, Contact>([SELECT Id,
        No_of_Open_Tasks__c FROM Contact WHERE Id in :contactIds]);


for(Contact con : contactMap.values()) {

con.No_of_Open_Tasks__c = 0;

}


for(AggregateResult ar : [SELECT WhoId, COUNT(Id) total FROM Task WHERE
IsClosed = false AND WhoId in :contactIds GROUP BY WhoId]) {

        String who = String.valueOf(ar.get('WhoId'));

        Decimal total = (Decimal)(ar.get('total'));

contactMap.get(who).No_of_Open_Tasks__c = total;
```

```
        }


        update contactMap.values();
    }
  }
}
```

We can save this code and test it through our user interface to check that it works as expected.

This was a far more detailed code example than we have seen before and covered off a number of key topics. I would recommend you spend time reading back through the final code version line by line again to cement the ideas as a lot of concepts have been covered. Before we finish with SOQL though we have a couple more areas to discuss.

# Querying relationships

Often we will want to query for related records to use within our processing. In other relational databases, this is achieved through the use of JOIN statements whereby multiple tables are joined together using foreign keys. As we saw in *Chapter 1: An Introduction to the Salesforce Platform*, Salesforce as a multitenant environment does not create a new table for each object we create, instead of using a simpler and more extensible structure to work with the metadata we define for the organization. As such, SOQL does not have the concept of a JOIN statement but instead uses relationship fields within queries to allow us to retrieve data from multiple objects at once.

When working with data and trying to retrieve information from related records we need to determine whether we are looking at data from a parent record (looking up the hierarchy) or retrieving child records (down the hierarchy). We also need to keep in mind whether the relationship is a standard or custom relationship.

# Data from parent records

Within a SOQL query, we can retrieve data from parent records by using the name of the lookup or master-detail field we have defined on our record. Let's look at an example using the standard account-contact relationship.

A contact looks up to an account using the `AccountId` field. This field holds the Id of the account that the contact record is related to, which is the 15 character case sensitive `Id` for the account record. In SOQL, if we wanted to retrieve a list of contacts with the first and last names, the contact record `Id` and the account record `Id` this would be:

```
[SELECT Id, FirstName, LastName, AccountId FROM Contact]
```

For standard relationship fields like this, there is a convention where you can access the parent record by using the parent object's name, or more generally, the relationship field without the `Id` suffix. For example, we can reference the `Id` and `Name` fields on our parent account record from our contact as:

```
[SELECT Id, FirstName, LastName, Account.Name, Account.Id FROM Contact]
```

Here `Acccount.Id` will return the same value as `AccountId` did before. Because when looking from child to parent we only have a single record, we can reference field values directly like this to allow us to retrieve related data.

For custom relationships, it is slightly different. Previously, we saw a custom invoice object which was the child or an opportunity. This was a custom relationship which we can see the definition for below:

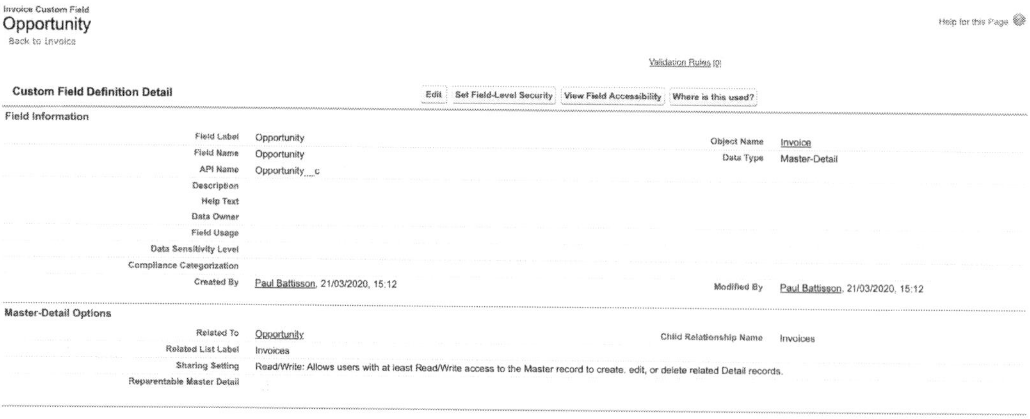

*Figure 7.6*

If we wanted to retrieve the opportunity's record `Id` and the invoice's `Name` we could do that as follows:

```
[SELECT Name, Opportunity__c FROM Invoice__c]
```

Here the data is stored in the custom `Opportunity__c` field which holds the 15 character record `Id` of the parent opportunity. For custom relationships, to retrieve data from the parent record, we need to change the `__c` suffix on the relationship field to a \_\_r. We can then access any fields on the parent object as we were doing before for the account, again using the dot notation:

```
[SELECT Name, Opportunity__r.Name, Opportunity__r.Amount FROM Invoice__c]
```

This is a really powerful piece of syntax as it enables us to retrieve information from parent records with no additional steps and makes it available to us as a field on the record that is returned through the same dot notation syntax we use to access fields on the record:

```
for(Invoice__c inv : [SELECT Name, Opportunity__r.Name, Opportunity__r.
Amount FROM Invoice__c]) {

System.debug('This invoice is related to the opportunity: ' + inv.
Opportunity__r.Name);

}
```

# Data from child records

We can also retrieve a list of child records as part of the query results set. We do this through the use of subqueries within our query.

In order to write a subquery, we need to know the child relationship name in order to use that as the object within the query syntax. We can see this name from the relationship field definition in the setup menu, as highlighted in the image below, the child relationship name is Contacts:

*Figure 7.7*

From our account record then we can add a subquery as follows to retrieve the first and last name of any contacts related to our account:

```
[SELECT Id, Name, (SELECT FirstName, LastName FROM Contacts) FROM Account]
```

As we can see, to define a subquery, you effectively construct the query as you would for retrieving the data from the child object, but replace the object name with the child relationship name. The subquery is then wrapped in parentheses and listed alongside the regular field list from the parent object. You can then access the list of contact records from the account record by using .Contacts as shown below:

```
for(Account acc : [SELECT Id, Name, (SELECT FirstName, LastName FROM
Contacts) FROM Account]) {

System.debug('For the account with name ' + acc.Name + ' I have the
following contacts:');

for(Contact con : acc.Contacts) { //acc.Contacts has type List<Contact>

System.debug(con.FirstName + ' ' + con.LastName);

}

}
```

The pattern is the same for custom relationships except that we again append a __r to the child relationship name:

```
[SELECT Name, (SELECT Name, Amount__c FROM Invoices__r) FROM Opportunity]
```

# Dynamic queries

The final thing for us to talk about in this section on SOQL is dynamic queries. There will be occasions where you may want to define the query to be run at run time, for example passing in a dynamic list of fields to be retrieved or taking in some input defined by a user through a search form.

You can run a query defined as a string using the Database.query method, for example:

```
Database.query('SELECT FirstName, LastName FROM Contact');
```

This can allow you to write more flexible applications where fields are retrieved based upon availability or through customization by an end-user. We can define fileds we wish to retrieve dynamically:

```
String fields = 'FirstName, LastName';

String queryString = 'SELECT ' + fields + ' FROM Contact';
```

```
List<Contact> contacts = Database.query(queryString);
```

In the above code we could generate the `fields` variable from some user provided input or other code. Simple bind variables are still available in dynamic SOQL queries:

```
String firstNameSearch; //This string is set by a user through a custom UI
```

```
List<Contact> contacts = Database.query('SELECT Id FROM Contact WHERE
FirstName = :firstNameSearch');
```

However, we cannot bind to fields in the query string:

```
Account myAcc; //An account record defined and populated earlier in the
code
```

```
List<Contact> contacts = Database.query('SELECT Id FROM Contact WHERE
AccountId = :myAcc.Id');
```

This query would not work and instead, you must retrieve the field value as a simple variable to bind to:

```
Id myAccId = myAcc.Id;
```

```
List<Contact> contacts = Database.query('SELECT Id FROM Contact WHERE
AccountId = :myAccId');
```

Finally, dynamic SOQL can open you to attacks via SOQL injection. This is where a malicious individual may try to inject code into the query to retrieve additional results. For example, if we had the query string:

```
String searchName; //Set by the user
```

```
List<Contact> contacts = Database.query('SELECT Id FROM Contact WHERE
FirstName LIKE \'%' + searchName + '%\'');
```

If a user enters `Mario` as the `searchName` value our query is:

```
SELECT Id FROM Contact WHERE FirstName LIKE 'Mario'
```

This is a valid query, however, they could enter the following:

```
test%' OR FirstName LIKE '
```

If the user enters this, our query is then evaluated as:

```
SELECT Id FROM Contact WHERE FirstName LIKE '%test%' OR FirstName LIKE '%'
```

This query would return all of our contact records and potentially open a data vulnerability. In order to defend against this, we would be better either running a static query:

```
String searchName; //Set by the user

List<Contact> contacts = [SELECT Id FROM Contact WHERE FirstName LIKE
:searchName];
```

Or if dynamic SOQL is definitively required then call the `escapeSingleQuotes` method to sanitize the input and escape any quotation marks:

```
String searchName; //Set by the user

List<Contact> contacts = Database.query('SELECT Id FROM Contact WHERE
FirstName LIKE \'%' + String.escapeSingleQuotes(searchName) + '%\'');
```

# Conclusion

This chapter has been a long a detailed one as we went through the many ways in which we can use the **Salesforce Object Query Language** (**SOQL**), to retrieve data from our database. We started by reviewing the differences between SOQL and SQL and saw how a SOQL query should be structured. We moved on to looking at how we can executed SOQL within Apex, how data is returned, and how we can use variables in our queries through binding.

We then looked at aggregate functions and grouping before working through a detailed trigger example that enabled us to use all these pieces together. We then wrapped up the chapter by looking through the use of relationships within queries to retrieve data from parent or child records, before finishing with a discussion around dynamic SOQL.

Now we understand SOQL, let's move ahead to the next chapter where we will be discussing its sister search language, SOSL.

# Questions

1. What does SOQL stand for?
2. How do we bind to a variable's values?
3. What type of data does a query return?
4. How can we retrieve data from a parent record in a query?
5. How can we retrieve child records in a query?
6. What should we be mindful of when writing dynamic SOQL?

# CHAPTER 8
# SOSL

In the last chapter, we learned about the **Salesforce Object Query Language** (**SOQL**). SOQL is a powerful tool for when we want to retrieve records from a known object and we know which fields we wish to query upon. Conversely, SOQL is not a great tool for when we are searching across multiple objects to find records matching a `String` value. For example, if you wanted to perform a text search across your leads and contacts for any reference to *widgets* this would involve a series of queries and complex filter logic to check the different combinations of fields.

To deliver this functionality in a simpler and more performant manner Salesforce provides the **Salesforce Object Search Language** (**SOSL**). SOSL allows developers to run a search against any text, URL, email, and phone fields across multiple objects simultaneously. You can thing of SOSL as a *Google search* for your objects.

## Structure

In this chapter we will cover:

- The structure of a SOSL search
- SOSL return types
- Filtering SOSL results
- When to use SOSL vs. SOQL

# Objectives

By the end of this chapter you should:

- Be able to write a SOSL search
- Know how to filter the return results from a SOSL search
- Know how to use the results from a SOSL search
- Know when to use SOSL vs. SOQL

# SOSL structure

SOSL searches have both a different structure and return type from SOQL queries. A SOSL statement is formatted as follows:

```
[FIND searchTerms IN searchGroup RETURNING objectListWithClauses]
```

Let's break these elements down one by one. The `searchTerms` are the strings we are searching for within our fields and can contain special characters and logic to enhance our searches. Some examples are:

- `'John'`: This will search for the word John specifically.
- `'J*n'`: The * asterisk acts as a wildcard and will match Jon, John, Jen, Jan, etc.
- `'J?n'`: The ? question mark will act as a single wildcard character only and here matches Jon, Jan, Jen but not John.
- `'John' OR 'Jane'`: We can use logical operators such as OR, AND, etc. to apply complex logic, here matching for John or Jane in our text.

The `searchGroup` portion of the statement defines which of the available field types we want to search and can have one of the following options:

- `ALL FIELDS`: This option searches all the available text fields for the values specified.
- `NAME FIELDS`: This option will search only the fields designated as name fields in the metadata.
- `EMAIL FIELDS`: This option will search only email type fields.
- `PHONE FIELDS`: This option will search only the phone type fields.

Finally, the `objectListWithClauses` defines the list of objects that will be searched and any clauses to apply to them. The simplest valid values here are just a list of sObjects that you wish to search and return matches from. For example, if we were searching for any opportunity records mentioning `widgets` our search would be:

```
[FIND 'widgets' IN ALL FIELDS RETURNING Opportunity];
```

If we run this in Apex, the return data type is different from our SOQL query return. Instead of returning a list with type List<sObject>, SOSL returns a data type List<List<sObject>>, that is a multi-dimensional list of records. This is because we can specify multiple objects to search across in our statement, for example:

```
List<List<sObject>> results = [FIND 'widgets' IN ALL FIELDS RETURNING Opportunity, Lead];
```

This search will look through all searchable fields on both the opportunity and lead objects and return lists of the matching results. In our results variable, the first List<sObject> in our List<List<sObject>> will be the matching opportunities and the second the matching leads:

```
List<List<sObject>> results = [FIND 'widgets' IN ALL FIELDS RETURNING Opportunity, Lead];


for(Opportunity opp : (List<Opportunity>)results[0]) {

System.debug(opp.Id);

}


for(Lead ld : (List<Lead>)results[1]) {

System.debug(ld.Id);

}
```

As you can see in this example, we have to cast the generic List<sObject> lists that are returned from the search but in doing so can then access the data within these records.

By default, this search will only return the Ids of records that meet the search criteria, in order to retrieve more fields you can list them within parentheses after the object name, for example:

```
List<List<sObject>> results = [FIND 'widgets' IN ALL FIELDS RETURNING Opportunity(Name, Amount), Lead(Name, Company)];


for(Opportunity opp : (List<Opportunity>)results[0]) {
```

```
System.debug('Matched ' + opp.Name + ' with value $' + opp.Amount);

}


for(Lead ld : (List<Lead>)results[1]) {

System.debug('Matched ' + ld.Name + ' from company ' + ld.Company);

}
```

This enables us to search retrieve a list of information to display back to the user or use within our Apex for processing even if they are not themselves included in the search. Similarly, we do not have to return all of the fields that were included in the search.

We can also add in WHERE clauses to the return information within our searches to enable us to filter the data being returned even further. For example, in our opportunity and lead search above, we only want to return open opportunities and leads that have not been marked as closed. We can do this through the use of filter criteria in the same way we did with SOQL:

```
List<List<sObject>> results = [FIND 'widgets' IN ALL FIELDS RETURNING
Opportunity(Name, Amount WHERE StageName != 'Closed Won' OR StageName !=
'Closed Lost'), Lead(Name, Company WHERE Status = 'Open - Not Contacted'
OR Status = 'Working - Contacted')];


for(Opportunity opp : (List<Opportunity>)results[0]) {

System.debug('Matched ' + opp.Name + ' with value $' + opp.Amount);

}


for(Lead ld : (List<Lead>)results[1]) {

System.debug('Matched ' + ld.Name + ' from company ' + ld.Company);

}
```

As we can see, it is easy for us to add criteria to the clauses in order to filter our data further. This can be extremely powerful in helping search results become more specific.

Often when developers implement search functionality through the use of SOSL they forget to include any prebuilt assumptions within the search that can give a poor user experience. In our example, it is likely that we were searching for opportunities and leads containing the word `widgets` to ensure they were receiving the latest marketing material, that the account manager or business development representative was aware of the new version of the widget, or to try and cross-sell a new product.

We will most likely not be interested in reaching out to opportunities that have been marked as closed won or lost as they would not benefit from this outreach. Similarly, leads are likely to only be applicable if they are actively being worked. These in-built assumptions apply additional filters that we can add to our searches through the use of filter criteria and enable us to provide a smaller result set as well as a better experience for our end users.

# Conclusion

This chapter on SOSL is relatively short as SOSL does not have the same level of depth in terms of features that we had with SOQL. However, SOSL is an extremely valuable tool when working in Apex to enable searching. As we discussed at the start of the chapter, whenever we are wanting to search across one or more records for a value in a text, phone, or email field we should look to SOSL instead of SOQL.

As we saw, SOSL is particularly useful when it comes to searching across multiple objects where we may not know which objects will contain matching records. Similarly, it has powerful features for wildcard matches and is able to work with languages such as Chinese, Japanese, Korean, or Thai as the inbuilt morphological tokenization can ensure accurate results are retrieved.

Finally, we saw how we can specify fields to be returned from the objects we are searching, as well as how to further filter the data using our `WHERE` clause syntax that we had previously seen. We also discussed how this can help us in providing a better experience for end-users and enable us to provide some assumptions into our searches to improve the results returned.

# Questions

1. When should we use SOSL instead of SOQL?
2. What data type does a SOSL search return in Apex?
3. How can I filter the results returned from a search?

# CHAPTER 9
# Apex Classes

Up until this point, we have focused largely on using Apex within a trigger context or through the execute anonymous window. We have for all intents and purposes, largely ignored the object-oriented aspects of Apex whilst hinting at them through things such as method calls and some constructors. In this chapter, we are now going to start diving into defining classes in Apex and how we can use some of the object-oriented features of the language to provide us some flexibility.

## Structure

In this chapter we will cover:

- Defining an Apex class
- Defining variables and properties
- Defining methods
- Using constructors
- Overloading methods and constructors
- Using inner classes

# Objectives

By the end of this chapter you should:

- Know how to define an Apex class
- Be able to add variables, properties, and methods to a class
- Know how the different access modifiers work
- Understand how to use the `static` keyword
- Be able to create custom constructors
- Understand when it may be appropriate to use inner classes

# Defining an Apex class

In their most basic form, Apex classes must have the following elements as part of their definition:

```
[global/public/private] [with/without sharing] class className          {



}
```

The first part of our definition is the choice of access modifier, either `global`, `public`, or `private`. The choice of access modifier here will affect what other code can access and use our class.

# Global

If we define the class with a `global` access modifier, this means that it can be seen by all Apex code within our org. This is useful for when are wanting to expose our code as a SOAP web service for use by other solutions, or when we are exposing an API for our solution for other developers to use. This is most commonly done by those publishing applications on the `appExchange` that may be integrated with.

# Public

A `public` access modifier declares that this class is visible to any code within the application or namespace. If we are working in a managed package environment then our code will be bundled in a namespace and locked to ensure intellectual property protection. If not in a managed package, the public access modifier simply ensures that the class can be called by the rest of the code within the organization.

# Private

When a class is given the `private` access modifier it must be either an inner class (that is a class defined within another class) or a test class (which we will discuss later). Classes designated `private` cannot be called outside of the class they are defined within.

Once we have defined the access for the class, we then define whether the class should run `with sharing` or `without sharing`. If we define the class as `with sharing`, Salesforce will enforce the sharing rules and sharing model for the current user running the code in the class to ensure that records that should not be visible are not retrieved as part of any queries that are made. This is important to ensure that our queries do not bring back any data the user should not have access to and therefore that it will not accidentally be shown to the user.

If we define a class as `without sharing` then we explicitly do not want the sharing rules and model to be applied to the code within that class meaning the class can access all data. This option should not be used by default as it invalidates the sharing model that has been defined for the environment and can lead to users seeing data they should not. There are use cases where this can be applied appropriately, for example in bulk or background asynchronous work, however by default all classes should be declared as `with sharing`.[1]

Finally, we give our class a name by populating the `className` portion of the definition. As a standard good practice, class names should be capitalized and if the class is performing a particular function, named to make this clear. Some examples are:

- `AccountUpdateUtility`: A class that contains a series of utility methods for working with an account update procedure.
- `ContactTriggerHandler`: A class that handles the trigger actions for the contact object.
- `LeadController`: A controller for some pages associated with the `Lead` object.

Giving classes meaningful names like this will help you and other developers to quickly understand what a class is doing and what methods should be within the class.

So, if we wanted to define a class that was a set of utility methods for our account object, we could define an `AccountUtility` class as follows:

---

1    There is an additional inherited sharing option, however it is an advanced technique and falls outside the scope of this book. In general developers should always declare classes as `with sharing`.

```
public with sharing AccountUtility {

    //class code goes here

}
```

This is a very basic class but one that is completely valid and can be used, although not for much. To make it more useful we will need to be able to enable the class to have some state and data to work with internally. For this, we are going to need to be able to define variables.

# Defining variables

Variables within classes can be thought of as attributes of the object it is describing. They are often referred to as member variables (i.e. variables for a specific member or instance of that class). For example, we may want to define a person as an object, in which case some of the following may be variables for the class:

- First Name
- Last Name
- Date of Birth
- Identification number (e.g. Social Security)

We define variables in classes in a similar fashion to how we define variables within code blocks, we provide their data type, a variable name, and then a value. It is common practice to do this at the top of the class. The only difference between variable declaration in a class and a code block is that within a class we provide an access modifier. In general, the declaration of a variable looks like:

```
[global/public/private/protected] dataType variableName[ = value];
```

Note we can either define the value of the variable on instantiation or leave it as `null` to be set later in the code.

Our accessors are similar to above; `private` limits access to the variable to only code within the class, `public` enables it to be accessed by any code within the application or namespace, `global` makes the variable visible to any code that can see the class. We also have a `protected` option. What does `protected` do?

We can think of the `protected` keyword is halfway between `private` and `public`. Items marked as `protected` can be accessed by any code within the class (much like a `private` variable), but also by any inner classes or extensions of the class in which it is defined. We will deal with inner classes in more detail later in the chapter, but we should be aware that `protected` provides us some benefits over both `public` and `private` for specific use cases.

Let us now return to the variables we mentioned for our person. We could define our `Person` class using the same format as we saw before:

```
public with sharing class Person {

}
```

We then define variables within the class as follows:

```
public with sharing class Person          {


    public String firstName;

    public String lastName;


    private Date dateOfBirth = Date.today();

    private String identification;

}
```

There are a few things we should pay attention to in this code. Firstly, note that I have grouped the `public` and `private` variables. This is a common convention to help make the code more readable and organized. Second, I have marked the `firstName` and `lastName` variables as public as these are all attributes that are visible about a person externally - it is hard to refer to someone without knowing their name. I have marked both `dateOfBirth` and `identification` as private as both of these are pieces of information we do not necessarily want to share. We have also defaulted our `dateOfBirth` to today's date (new `Person` instances can be considered to be born today - we will look at how to overwrite that later).

In general, you should think carefully when defining classes about encapsulation, that is the process of only exposing data and methods which need to be available outside of the class as `public` and hiding other information. This is a best practice to ensure that we do not have data leaking between objects unnecessarily which can lead to code being fragile through assumptions and unexpected consequences.

# Defining properties

Properties differ from member variables in that they expose data outside of a class but can have additional code logic or side effects as part of their definition and retrieval. Let us take an example of our age. The `Person` class we have defined stores our date of birth as a `private` variable meaning it cannot be accessed outside the class. Suppose we had some other logic that required the age of the `Person` instance, for example, determining if they were an adult. For this, we could expose our age as a property.

Properties have a `get` and a `set` accessor (often referred to as a getter or setter). These are blocks of code that are executed whenever the property is retrieved or assigned a value respectively. A property is defined as follows:

```
[global/public/private/protected] dataType propertyName {

    get {

        //code run when property is read

    }

    set {

        //code run when property is assigned a value

    }

}
```

We do not have to provide any blocks of code at all if we wanted an automatic property, for example, if we wanted to declare a public `String` property that holds a message:

```
public String message {get; set;}
```

If we wanted to make a property read-only to an external class, we can also define the setter to be `private`, meaning the value can only be set by the class:

```
public String messageReadOnly {get; private set;}
```

Let's look at defining our age as a property of the `Person` class. We know that our age is the difference between today and our date of birth, divided by 365 and rounded to the nearest whole number. We do not want our age to be writeable and so we will use a `private` setter:

```
public with sharing class Person {


    public String firstName;

    public String lastName;
```

```
public String sex;


private Date dateOfBirth = Date.today();

private String identification;


public Integer age {

    get {

        return Math.ceil((Date.today() - dateOfBirth)/365);

    }

    private set;

}
```

```
}
```

The Math.ceil function here takes the decimal value returned from our calculation and rounds down to the nearest integer providing us the number of whole years.

# Why do we need properties?

At this point, you may be wondering why we need both properties and variables. What is the difference?

Both properties and variables can be accessed via the dot notation:

```
Person john; //A person instance called john defined previously in our code

john.firstName; // Retrieves "John"

john.age; //Returns 43 for example
```

So to our external code, there is little difference. The main differences are the ability to do other work before retrieving/setting a value, as we have already seen, and the ability to bind.

If we are working with a Visualforce page and wish to display some data from an Apex class (referred to as a controller) then we need to expose the data we wish to display as a property in the controller class for display on the page. It is outside the scope of this book to go into working with Visualforce, but it is important that we mention this use case as it is often a point of confusion for new developers as to why you may have properties or what they do when you encounter them in a Visualforce page. You will still find many good use cases for properties within non-Visualforce code, but it is in working with Visualforce where you will encounter a greater proportion of properties being used.

# Defining methods

Throughout the book, we have seen a number of examples of calling methods, most notably the `debug()` method on the `System` class in the form `System.debug('My string')`. How do we define methods for our classes for us to then call?

Method definition in Apex follows a standard format:

```
[global/public/private/protected] returnType methodName(optionalParamType optionalParamName) {

    //method body

}
```

Our access modifiers are the same as we had before and have the same implications as they did on our variables. The `returnType` is the datatype of the value we are returning from our method. If we are not returning any data at all then we use the special return type `void` keyword. We give our method a name and then have a set of parentheses with one or more parameters listed that we can pass in for the method to use.

Let's look at an example method. If I wanted to define a method that given two integers adds them together and returns their sum, I could define my add method as:

```
public Integer add(Integer item1, Integer item2) {

    return item1 + item2;

}
```

I could place this inside a `Calculator` class:

```
public with sharing class Calculator {

    public Integer add(Integer item1, Integer item2) {

        return item1 + item2;

    }
```

```
}
```

If I then had an instance of my `Calculator` class called `calc` I could add two integers as:

```
Integer total = calc.add(5, 6); //Total is set to 11
```

As we can see we call methods using the *dot* notation, `class.method()`, in the same way, we access variables using `class.variable`. We use the `return` keyword to end the method execution and return the value of the expression that follows. This can be used multiple times within different logic branches in a method to ensure that correct data is always returned or to finish a method early once the correct data to return has been generated, for example:

```
public with sharing class Calculator {

    public Integer add(Integer item1, Integer item2) {

if(item1 == null || item2 == null) {

        return 0;

    }

    return item1 + item2;

    }

}
```

In this example we return 0 if either of the numbers passed in is `null` and exit the method early, otherwise, we perform the necessary calculation.

# Don't Repeat Yourself (DRY)

Many books have been written, and many more still will be, about the best way in which to structure your code and methods within classes. I want to briefly touch on the approach I have found has worked best for me, and that is to simply try and keep my code **DRY** - that is **Don't Repeat Yourself**.

I bring this up here because when we start discussing method declaration, it is easy to see how you can utilize `public` methods within your code, but it is less clear often how you can utilize `private` methods. In general, `private` methods are used for one of the following reasons:

- To provide a single reusable method for repeated code. This minimizes the number of times we would need to update this could should it need to change and helps us avoid errors.

- To hide details or actions from the code calling our class that it does not need to see.

For example, if we had a `Clock` class, we may have public methods `getCurrentTime` and `setCorrectTime` and a `private` method `formatTime` which will be used by these methods to change the time between 12 and 24-hour formats.

My advice for new developers is to extract repeated code into a `private` method within your class whenever possible to help keep your code DRY. As you do this, you will start to notice when you have instances of code that could be extracted into `private` methods, and when it makes sense to have code encapsulated away correctly.

# Class constructors

We have seen previously how we can create instances of `sObjects` such as

```
Account acc = new Account();
```

What we haven't covered in too much detail is what the `newAccount()` portion of this code is doing.

When we use the `new` keyword, we tell the system we wish to create a new instance of an object for the given data type. When we then make the `Account()` call, we are calling the default constructor on the `Account sObject` class.

A constructor is a special type of method that is called before returning the object instance. Every class in Apex comes with a default constructor that takes in no parameters. So if we wanted to create a new instance of our `Person` class we could simply call the default constructor:

```
Person jane = new Person();
```

This provides us with an instance of our `Person` class to work with. We can define some code to run in the constructor by explicitly defining the constructor in our class definition:

```
public with sharing class Person {

    public String firstName;

    public String lastName;

    public String sex;
```

```
    private Date dateOfBirth = Date.today();

    private String identification;


    public Integer age {

        get {

            return Math.ceil((Date.today() - dateOfBirth)/365);

        }

        private set;

    }


    public Person() {
firstName = 'John'; //default the first name to John

lastName = 'Doe'; //default the last name to Doe

    }

}
```

Now when we create our new Person instance the values of John and Doe are populated by default:

```
Person jane = new Person();

jane.firstName; //returns "John"

jane.lastName; //returns "Doe"
```

We can take in parameters as part of our constructor, and provide multiple constructors for our class to enable us to create instances in multiple ways, for example:

```
public with sharing class Person {


    public String firstName;

    public String lastName;

    public String sex;
```

```apex
    private Date dateOfBirth = Date.today();

    private String identification;


    public Integer age {
        get {
            return Math.ceil((Date.today() - dateOfBirth)/365);
        }
        private set;
    }


    public Person() {
firstName = 'John'; //default the first name to John

lastName = 'Doe'; //default the last name to Doe

    }


    public Person(String first, String last) {
firstName = first;

lastName = last;

    }


}
```

Now we have a second constructor that we can use which enables us to create instances of our Person class and provide them a first and last name:

```apex
Person jane = new Person('Jane', 'Smith');

jane.firstName; //returns "Jane"

jane.lastName; //returns "Smith"
```

It should be noted that as soon as we define a custom constructor, we lose the default constructor and have to explicitly declare it to use it.

# this keyword

In some examples and code you would see the new constructor we wrote as:

```
public Person(String first, String last) {

this.firstName = first;

this.lastName = last;

}
```

The `this` keyword is a special keyword that refers to the current instance of our `Apex` class. When we call `this.firstName` it refers to the `firstName` variable within the instance of the class we are currently in and can be useful when working with extensions of classes.

Another use case for the `this` keyword is in constructor chaining. Within a constructor we can use the `this` keyword to call another constructor to generate the class, for example, we could rewrite our constructors as:

```
public Person() {

this('John', 'Doe'); //this will call the constructor below with our
values.

        }


public Person(String first, String last) {

firstName = first;

lastName = last;

}
```

This can be an extremely effective technique to allow you to default values and generate new instances of classes.

# Overloading methods

The technical name for what we have done with our constructors above is *overloading*, that is we have provided multiple versions of the same thing with different parameters. We can also do this with the methods we have declared in our classes. To do this we simply declare the same method but with a different set of parameters. An example might be:

```
public Account createAccount() {

    return createAccount('Default');

}


public Account createAccount(String name) {

    Account acc = new Account();

acc.Name = name;

    return acc;

}
```

This is a typical example of code for use in creating test data for unit tests, a topic we will discuss in more detail later.

This behavior is also called *polymorphism* and just means that we can define our method multiple times in different ways to enable us to call it appropriately. Another benefit of coding in this manner is again we can reduce the amount of repetition in our code and keep it DRY. In the example above, if a new required field was added to the Account object, we could simply update the code once and the rest of our overloaded methods would also work.

# Static methods, variables, and blocks

We have now seen how we can define a class and create a new instance of it in our Apex code. Some of the methods we have used before however, such as System. debug() have not required us to create a new instance of the class before we have utilized the method. Methods such as this are called static methods, and the static keyword can be used to provide variables and methods that do not need an instance of the class created before they are utilized.

Let us go back to our Calculator class. When we create an instance of a class we are doing so because the object we create will hold some state that we want to maintain. We don't have any state that we will want our Calculator class to hold, so we don't need to have an instance of it. When we add two numbers, we do not need to store the state of this anywhere.

We could, therefore, redefine our `Calculator` class as follows:

```
public with sharing class Calculator        {



    public static Integer add(Integer item1, Integer item2) {
if(item1 == null || item2 == null) {

        return 0;

    }

    return item1 + item2;

        }



}
```

We add the `static` keyword before the return type from our method definition to indicate to the rest of our code that we can call this method without the need to have an instance of the class.

To call our new add method then is simply:

```
Integer total = Calculator.add(7, 6);
```

When it comes to defining variables as `static`, the variable will exist for the entirety of the Apex transaction and can, therefore, be used to either cache values throughout the transaction or allow you as a developer to manage the execution of your code across the transaction. For example, we may have some data in a custom metadata type that we want to refer to in our code. A common pattern is to have a utility class to retrieve this data once and store it in a variable for use across the transaction:

```
public with sharing class MyMetadataUtility {


    private static My_Metadata__mdt myMetadata;


    public static My_Metadata__mdt getMyMetadata() {
if(myMetadata == null) {
```

```
myMetadata = [SELECT Id, Name FROM My_Metadata__mdt LIMIT 1];

    }


    return myMetadata;

  }

}
```

This code will retrieve the custom metadata record at most once per transaction when the getMyMetadata method is called and store the My_Metadata__mdt record returned in the myMetadataprivatestatic variable for repeated use should the getMyMetadata method be called again.

We can also define a static initialization block of code. That is a block of code within our class that is called the first time a class is accessed and is not run afterward. Our previous example could be updated to:

```
public with sharing class MyMetadataUtility {


    private static My_Metadata__mdt myMetadata;


    static {
myMetadata = [SELECT Id, Name FROM My_Metadata__mdt LIMIT 1];
    }


    public static My_Metadata__mdt getMyMetadata() {
        return myMetadata;
    }

}
```

This static block will be run the first time that the class is accessed and will populate myMetadata. Every subsequent time, the class is accessed within the transaction it will not be called.

# final variables

There are instances where we will want to define variables and have the value set so that it cannot be changed. To do this we can use the final keyword during our variable declaration. The final keyword indicates that the variable can only be defined as a value once, with when the variable is declared or within a constructor. For example:

```
public with sharing class Example {


    public final String setOnDeclaration = 'value set on declaration';

    public final String setinConstructor;


    public Example() {
setinConstructor = 'value set in constructor';

    }


}
```

We can also mark a variable as both static and final, creating a constant:

```
private static final Integer DAYS_IN_YEAR = 365;
```

Constants in this form can also be set on declaration or in static initialization blocks. Note that it is a common practice to capitalize constants and use underscores as spaces for code readability.

# Inner classes

When we discussed the protected keyword earlier in the chapter we mentioned that it makes methods and variables visible to inner classes and extensions. We will discuss extensions in the next chapter, but what is an inner class?

An inner class is a class defined within another class. We define an inner class by simply defining a class within an existing class:

```
public with sharing class MyClass {
```

```
public with sharing class MyInnerClass {



    }

}
```

We can refer to this class using dot notation as `MyClass.MyInnerClass` as the inner class is also `public`. It should be noted that the inner class does not inherit sharing from the outer class.

Inner classes typically have 3 use cases, to keep our code DRY, to be used as a wrapper for selection or for deserialization. Let us review each of these use cases.

# Keeping code DRY

We may use inner classes to encapsulate some of our functionality in a way that helps us to keep our code DRY and easier to work with. An example might be if we had a Book class that we were working with. A book has a number of chapters that make it up. As a chapter only makes sense as part of a book, we could create a `Chapter` inner class that holds the details of a book's chapter. In code this may look like:

```
public with sharing class Book {

    public String title;

    public List<Chapter> chapters = new List<Chapter>();


    public with sharing class Chapter {

        public String title;

        public Integer numberOfPages;


        public Chapter(String chapterTitle, Integer numPages) {

            title = chapterTitle;
numberOfPages = numPages;

        }

    }
```

```
}
```

We could then generate our book and add some chapters as follows:

```
Book learningApex = new Book();

learningApex.title = 'Learning Salesforce Development With Apex';

learningApex.chapters.add(new Book.Chapter('Apex Classes', 25);
```

This structures our code well and allows us to group functionality together appropriately.

# Selection wrappers

When working with records in a custom user interface there will be instances where you wish to present a list of records with the ability to select one or many of them using a checkbox, much like the standard list view. A common pattern to enable this is the use of a selection wrapper inner class. For example, if we had a list of contacts we wished to do this for, our class may look something like:

```
public with sharing class ContactListController {


    //define a public property for our list of wrappers that the UI can use

    public List<ContactWrapper> contacts {get; set;}


    //an example constructor to retrieve some contacts to populate our list

    public ContactListController() {

        contacts = new List<ContactWrapper>();
for(Contact con : SELECT Id, FirstName, LastName FROM Contact LIMIT 20]) {
contacts.add(new ContactWrapper(con));

        }

    }


//an example action method, this would be called from a button on the UI
public PageReference updateSelected() {
```

```
for(ContactWrapper wrapper : contacts) {

        //this would debug whether for each of our wrappers the checkbox
        bound to the "selected" Boolean had been checked

System.debug(wrapper.con.FirstName + ' ' + wrapper.con.LastName + ' is
selected? ' + wrapper.selected);

    }

  }


    //our inner wrapper class stores the Contact instance and a Boolean
    indicating it has been selected

    public with sharing class ContactWrapper {

        public Boolean selected {get; set;}

        public Contact con {get; set;}


        public ContactWrapper(Contact cont) {

            selected = false;

            con = cont;

        }

    }



}
```

The `ContactWrapper`inner class we define hold both a Contact record insatcne and a `Boolean` value indicating whether or not the record has been selected from the list. This checkbox does not exist on the record itself, but we use our ContactWrapperto provide an additional property for use in this instance.

This pattern is very common when working with user interfaces. Working with a UI is outside the scope of this book however the above code could be used as a Visualforce controller that would allow you to select one or more contacts from a list.

# Deserialization

The other common use case for inner classes is to assist in deserializing data returned from a web service call. When working with web services we will often receive back blobs of data, often in a JSON format, that we need to appropriately parse into Apex for us to work with. For example, we may get the following data returned from an API for us to work with:

```
{

    "orderId" : "123456",

    "productSKU" : "XXTBG163",

    "quantity" : 5,

    "unitPrice" : 99.97,

    "account" : "ACME_88987"

}
```

This data contains a mix of data types and would be hard to cast to a generic set of primitives. We a defined format like this we can build an inner class as part of our class that is parsing the JSON to handle this:

```
public with sharing class MyCalloutClass        {

    public with sharing class OrderWrapper {

        public String orderId;

        public String productSKU;

        public Integer quantity;

        public Double unitPrice;

        public String accountId;

        }


}
```

We could then deserialize our JSON string into the `OrderWrapper` class type and work with the results more readily. We will discuss this further in *Chapter 12: Callouts in Apex* when we look at making web service callouts.

# A detailed example

Now we understand how to define a class, methods, and variables, let's build out a more detailed example. In this example, we are going to take the code we had from our `TaskTrigger` in *Chapter 7: SOQL* and extract it to a utility class.

This is a common pattern called a trigger handler and allows us to extract the code that we run within our trigger into a class so that it is easier to manage and maintain. It also assists us in adhering to the *one trigger per object* best practice that can help ensure our code runs in a repeatable manner. Finally, it can also make our code easier to test. The implementation we are putting in place here is the most simplistic of trigger handler setups and much better tried and tested variations exist for production implementation.

We can recall our `TaskTrigger` code is as follows:

```
trigger TaskTrigger on Task (after insert, after update) {

    switch on Trigger.operationType {

        when AFTER_INSERT {

            Set<Id> contactIds = new Set<Id>();

for(Task t : Trigger.new) {

if(t.WhoId != null && String.valueOf(t.WhoId).startsWith('003')) {

contactIds.add(t.WhoId);

            }

        }


    Map<Id, Contact> contactMap = new Map<Id, Contact>([SELECT Id, No_of_
    Open_Tasks__c FROM Contact WHERE Id in :contactIds]);


for(Task t : Trigger.new) {

if(contactMap.containsKey(t.WhoId)) {

contactMap.get(t.WhoId).No_of_Open_Tasks__c += 1;

        }
```

```
        }


        update contactMap.values();

    }

    when AFTER_UPDATE {

        Set<Id> contactIds = new Set<Id>();

for(Task t : Trigger.new) {

if(t.IsClosed && !Trigger.oldMap.get(t.Id).IsClosed && t.WhoId != null &&
String.valueOf(t.WhoId).startsWith('003')) {

contactIds.add(t.WhoId);

            }

        }



    Map<Id, Contact> contactMap = new Map<Id, Contact>([SELECT Id, No_of_
    Open_Tasks__c FROM Contact WHERE Id in :contactIds]);


for(Contact con : contactMap.values()) {

con.No_of_Open_Tasks__c = 0;

        }



    for(AggregateResult ar : [SELECT WhoId, COUNT(Id) total FROM Task
    WHERE IsClosed = false AND WhoId in :contactIds GROUP BY WhoId]) {

        String who = String.valueOf(ar.get('WhoId'));

        Decimal total = (Decimal)(ar.get('total'));

contactMap.get(who).No_of_Open_Tasks__c = total;

        }



        update contactMap.values();
```

```
        }

    }

}
```

Let's start by declaring a new Apex class in the Developer Console using the **File** menu option, selecting **New Apex Class**, and entering `TaskTriggerHandler` as the name for our new Apex class. This is a commonly used naming convention for trigger handler classes within the Salesforce ecosystem. Our base class now looks as follows:

```
public class TaskTriggerHandler                                            {


}
```

As a best practice, we should first update the code to include a without sharing definition:

```
public without sharing class TaskTriggerHandler {


}
```

This time we are going to declare `without sharing` as our code is going to be querying and aggregating records that the user may not own or have visibility to (the `Task` records). Using `without` sharing will mean our totals will still be correct.

In our trigger, we have 2 contexts we are dealing with, `after insert` and `after update`. It makes logical sense then to define 2 methods for our class that will deal with these separate contexts:

```
public without sharing class TaskTriggerHandler {


    public void afterInsert() {


    }


    public void afterUpdate() {
```

```
        }


}
```

If we were to take the code within the after insert context and copy it into our class, we would have the following:

```
public without sharing class TaskTriggerHandler {


    public void afterInsert() {
        Set<Id> contactIds = new Set<Id>();
for(Task t : Trigger.new) {
if(t.WhoId != null && String.valueOf(t.WhoId).startsWith('003')) {
contactIds.add(t.WhoId);

        }
    }


    Map<Id, Contact> contactMap = new Map<Id, Contact>([SELECT Id, No_of_
    Open_Tasks__c FROM Contact WHERE Id in :contactIds]);


for(Task t : Trigger.new) {
if(contactMap.containsKey(t.WhoId)) {
contactMap.get(t.WhoId).No_of_Open_Tasks__c += 1;

        }
    }


    update contactMap.values();
        }
```

```
    public void afterUpdate() {



        }



}
```

If we start reading through this code to see if it will compile and run, we notice that we have the `Trigger.new` context variable being called within our loops. If this code is running in a trigger context, which it will be, it has access to these variables, however, I am going to propose to make our testing easier we add a parameter to our `afterInsert` method which is of type `List<Task>` and will be used in place of `Trigger.new`. Within our trigger code, we can simply pass in `Trigger.new`, but it will make the code less tightly coupled to the trigger context and so easier to test. We should then replace our instances of `Trigger.new` with this new list parameter, which will leave our updated code looks like:

```
public without sharing class TaskTriggerHandler {


    public void afterInsert(List<Task> newTasks) {
        Set<Id> contactIds = new Set<Id>();
for(Task t : newTasks) {
if(t.WhoId != null && String.valueOf(t.WhoId).startsWith('003')) {
contactIds.add(t.WhoId);
        }
    }


    Map<Id, Contact> contactMap = new Map<Id, Contact>([SELECT Id, No_of_
    Open_Tasks__c FROM Contact WHERE Id in :contactIds]);


for(Task t : newTasks) {
if(contactMap.containsKey(t.WhoId)) {
contactMap.get(t.WhoId).No_of_Open_Tasks__c += 1;
```

```
            }
        }


        update contactMap.values();
    }


    public void afterUpdate() {


    }


}
```

We can then update our trigger as well to look as follows:

```
trigger TaskTrigger on Task (after insert, after update) {
    switch on Trigger.operationType {
when AFTER_INSERT {
TaskTriggerHandler handler = new TaskTriggerHandler();
handler.afterInsert((List<Task>)Trigger.new);
        }
        when AFTER_UPDATE {
            Set<Id> contactIds = new Set<Id>();
for(Task t : Trigger.new) {
if(t.IsClosed && !Trigger.oldMap.get(t.Id).IsClosed && t.WhoId != null &&
String.valueOf(t.WhoId).startsWith('003')) {
contactIds.add(t.WhoId);
            }
            }
```

```
Map<Id, Contact> contactMap = new Map<Id, Contact>([SELECT Id, No_of_
Open_Tasks__c FROM Contact WHERE Id in :contactIds]);


for(Contact con : contactMap.values()) {

con.No_of_Open_Tasks__c = 0;

      }



for(AggregateResult ar : [SELECT WhoId, COUNT(Id) total FROM Task WHERE
IsClosed = false AND WhoId in :contactIds GROUP BY WhoId]) {

        String who = String.valueOf(ar.get('WhoId'));

        Decimal total = (Decimal)(ar.get('total'));

contactMap.get(who).No_of_Open_Tasks__c = total;

      }



        update contactMap.values();

     }

   }

}
```

I am also explicitly casting the data in `Trigger.new` to a type `List<Task>` when we make our method call to make things clear and avoid any conversion errors.

We can now repeat the process we have just followed for our `after update` context, copying the code across as follows:

```
public void afterUpdate() {

    Set<Id> contactIds = new Set<Id>();

for(Task t : Trigger.new) {

if(t.IsClosed && !Trigger.oldMap.get(t.Id).IsClosed && t.WhoId != null &&
String.valueOf(t.WhoId).startsWith('003')) {

contactIds.add(t.WhoId);
```

```
      }
   }


   Map<Id, Contact> contactMap = new Map<Id, Contact>([SELECT Id, No_of_
   Open_Tasks__c FROM Contact WHERE Id in :contactIds]);


for(Contact con : contactMap.values()) {
con.No_of_Open_Tasks__c = 0;
   }


for(AggregateResult ar : [SELECT WhoId, COUNT(Id) total FROM Task WHERE
IsClosed = false AND WhoId in :contactIds GROUP BY WhoId]) {
      String who = String.valueOf(ar.get('WhoId'));
      Decimal total = (Decimal)(ar.get('total'));
contactMap.get(who).No_of_Open_Tasks__c = total;
   }


   update contactMap.values();
}
```

If we look again for our `trigger` variables, we will see that we are using both `Trigger.new` and `Trigger.oldMap` and so to decouple our code should pass these in as parameters and replace our trigger instance variables:

```
public void afterUpdate(List<Task> newTasks, Map<Id, Task> oldTaskMap) {
   Set<Id> contactIds = new Set<Id>();
for(Task t : newTasks) {
if(t.IsClosed && !oldTaskMap.get(t.Id).IsClosed && t.WhoId != null &&
String.valueOf(t.WhoId).startsWith('003')) {
contactIds.add(t.WhoId);
```

```
        }
    }



    Map<Id, Contact> contactMap = new Map<Id, Contact>([SELECT Id, No_of_
    Open_Tasks__c FROM Contact WHERE Id in :contactIds]);



for(Contact con : contactMap.values()) {

con.No_of_Open_Tasks__c = 0;

    }



for(AggregateResult ar : [SELECT WhoId, COUNT(Id) total FROM Task WHERE
IsClosed = false AND WhoId in :contactIds GROUP BY WhoId]) {

        String who = String.valueOf(ar.get('WhoId'));

        Decimal total = (Decimal)(ar.get('total'));

contactMap.get(who).No_of_Open_Tasks__c = total;

    }



    update contactMap.values();

}
```

Our updated trigger and trigger handler should now look like the following:

```
trigger TaskTrigger on Task (after insert, after update) {
    switch on Trigger.operationType {
        when AFTER_INSERT {
TaskTriggerHandler handler = new TaskTriggerHandler();

handler.afterInsert((List<Task>)Trigger.new);

        }
        when AFTER_UPDATE {
```

```
TaskTriggerHandler handler = new TaskTriggerHandler();

handler.afterUpdate((List<Task>)Trigger.new,    (Map<Id,    Task>)Trigger.
oldMap);

        }

    }

}

public without sharing class TaskTriggerHandler {


    public void afterInsert(List<Task> newTasks) {

        Set<Id> contactIds = new Set<Id>();

for(Task t : newTasks) {

if(t.WhoId != null && String.valueOf(t.WhoId).startsWith('003')) {

contactIds.add(t.WhoId);

        }

    }


    Map<Id, Contact> contactMap = new Map<Id, Contact>([SELECT Id, No_of_
    Open_Tasks__c FROM Contact WHERE Id in :contactIds]);


for(Task t : newTasks) {

if(contactMap.containsKey(t.WhoId)) {

contactMap.get(t.WhoId).No_of_Open_Tasks__c += 1;

        }

    }


    update contactMap.values();

    }
```

```
    public void afterUpdate(List<Task> newTasks, Map<Id, Task> oldTaskMap) {

        Set<Id> contactIds = new Set<Id>();

for(Task t : newTasks) {

if(t.IsClosed && !oldTaskMap.get(t.Id).IsClosed && t.WhoId != null &&
String.valueOf(t.WhoId).startsWith('003')) {

contactIds.add(t.WhoId);

        }

    }


    Map<Id, Contact> contactMap = new Map<Id, Contact>([SELECT Id, No_of_
    Open_Tasks__c FROM Contact WHERE Id in :contactIds]);


for(Contact con : contactMap.values()) {

con.No_of_Open_Tasks__c = 0;

        }


for(AggregateResult ar : [SELECT WhoId, COUNT(Id) total FROM Task WHERE
IsClosed = false AND WhoId in :contactIds GROUP BY WhoId]) {

        String who = String.valueOf(ar.get('WhoId'));

        Decimal total = (Decimal)(ar.get('total'));

contactMap.get(who).No_of_Open_Tasks__c = total;

    }


        update contactMap.values();

    }


}
```

This has kept our trigger leaner and cleaner making it far easier to deal with and has also decoupled the code for our trigger so that we could run the code for testing without a need to execute the trigger (we will discuss the value of this more in *Chapter 11: Testing Apex* when we discuss Apex testing). Could we improve this code further?

Firstly, we have our contact prefix key hardcoded in 2 places within the code. As we mentioned previously in *Chapter 6: Apex Triggers*, we can be comfortable that the prefix for the contact will remain 003 as it is a Salesforce standard object, however, good practice would still dictate that we should retrieve it dynamically if it is simple (which it is) and it will also allow us to see the method for doing this so that we are aware in other situations. This is also a good use of a constant within our class as we are only wanting the value set once and do not change throughout the transaction. We would define our new constant as:

```
private static final String KEY_PREFIX = Contact.sObjectType.getDescribe().
getKeyPrefix();
```

Again, the process here of calling multiple methods in a single statement is called chaining and allows us to work across a number of objects easily. The `Contact.sObjectType` property here returns an instance of the `SObjectType` class which has a method called `getDescribe()`. This in turn returns an instance of the `DescribeSObjectResult` class which has a method `getKeyPrefix()` which returns our key prefix for the sObject - in this case, 003.

We should place this declaration at the top of our class and replace any instances of 003 with it:

```
public without sharing class TaskTriggerHandler {


    private    static    final    String    KEY_PREFIX    =    Contact.sObjectType.
    getDescribe().getKeyPrefix();


    public void afterInsert(List<Task> newTasks) {

        Set<Id> contactIds = new Set<Id>();

for(Task t : newTasks) {

if(t.WhoId != null && String.valueOf(t.WhoId).startsWith(KEY_PREFIX)) {

contactIds.add(t.WhoId);

        }
```

```
    }


    Map<Id, Contact> contactMap = new Map<Id, Contact>([SELECT Id, No_of_
    Open_Tasks__c FROM Contact WHERE Id in :contactIds]);


    for(Task t : newTasks) {

    if(contactMap.containsKey(t.WhoId)) {

    contactMap.get(t.WhoId).No_of_Open_Tasks__c += 1;

        }

      }


    update contactMap.values();

  }


    public void afterUpdate(List<Task> newTasks, Map<Id, Task> oldTaskMap) {

        Set<Id> contactIds = new Set<Id>();
    for(Task t : newTasks) {

    if(t.IsClosed && !oldTaskMap.get(t.Id).IsClosed && t.WhoId != null &&
    String.valueOf(t.WhoId).startsWith(KEY_PREFIX)) {

    contactIds.add(t.WhoId);

        }

      }


    Map<Id, Contact> contactMap = new Map<Id, Contact>([SELECT Id, No_of_
    Open_Tasks__c FROM Contact WHERE Id in :contactIds]);


  for(Contact con : contactMap.values()) {

  con.No_of_Open_Tasks__c = 0;
```

```
    }


for(AggregateResult ar : [SELECT WhoId, COUNT(Id) total FROM Task WHERE
IsClosed = false AND WhoId in :contactIds GROUP BY WhoId]) {

    String who = String.valueOf(ar.get('WhoId'));

    Decimal total = (Decimal)(ar.get('total'));

contactMap.get(who).No_of_Open_Tasks__c = total;

    }


    update contactMap.values();

    }


}
```

The statement where we are using the KEY_PREFIX variable is also slightly cumbersome to read and is being used in multiple places, we could extract that to a method as well to make our code neater:

```
public without sharing class TaskTriggerHandler {


    private static final String KEY_PREFIX = Contact.sObjectType.
    getDescribe().getKeyPrefix();


    private Boolean isContactId(Id recordId) {

        return String.valueOf(recordId).startsWith(KEY_PREFIX);

    }


    public void afterInsert(List<Task> newTasks) {

        Set<Id> contactIds = new Set<Id>();
for(Task t : newTasks) {
```

```
if(t.WhoId != null && isContactId(t.WhoId)) {

contactIds.add(t.WhoId);

        }

    }


    Map<Id, Contact> contactMap = new Map<Id, Contact>([SELECT Id, No_of_
    Open_Tasks__c FROM Contact WHERE Id in :contactIds]);


for(Task t : newTasks) {

if(contactMap.containsKey(t.WhoId)) {

contactMap.get(t.WhoId).No_of_Open_Tasks__c += 1;

            }

        }


    update contactMap.values();

    }


    public void afterUpdate(List<Task> newTasks, Map<Id, Task> oldTaskMap) {

        Set<Id> contactIds = new Set<Id>();

for(Task t : newTasks) {

if(t.IsClosed && !oldTaskMap.get(t.Id).IsClosed && t.WhoId != null &&
isContactId(t.WhoId)) {

contactIds.add(t.WhoId);

        }

    }


    Map<Id, Contact> contactMap = new Map<Id, Contact>([SELECT Id, No_of_
    Open_Tasks__c FROM Contact WHERE Id in :contactIds]);
```

```
for(Contact con : contactMap.values()) {

con.No_of_Open_Tasks__c = 0;

    }


for(AggregateResult ar : [SELECT WhoId, COUNT(Id) total FROM Task WHERE
IsClosed = false AND WhoId in :contactIds GROUP BY WhoId]) {

      String who = String.valueOf(ar.get('WhoId'));

      Decimal total = (Decimal)(ar.get('total'));

contactMap.get(who).No_of_Open_Tasks__c = total;

      }


      update contactMap.values();

    }


}
```

Our new isContactId method is private as external code does not need to see it and helps the remainder of our code become easier to read. Note that the startsWith method we are calling returns a Boolean value and so we can simply return that rather than having to assign the value to a variable and then return it.

So far we have just been following our DRY principles in helping us to decide how to structure our class. The only other location we have duplicated code in this class now is the retrieval of the contact data via our query. We could also extract this to a simple method to again make the code more readable and have a single query to update in our code going forward:

```
public without sharing class TaskTriggerHandler {


  private static final String KEY_PREFIX = Contact.sObjectType.
  getDescribe().getKeyPrefix();
```

```
    private Boolean isContactId(Id recordId) {

        return String.valueOf(recordId).startsWith(KEY_PREFIX);

    }


    private Map<Id, Contact> retrieveContacts(Set<Id> contactIds) {

        return new Map<Id, Contact>([SELECT Id, No_of_Open_Tasks__c FROM
        Contact WHERE Id in :contactIds]);

    }


    public void afterInsert(List<Task> newTasks) {

        Set<Id> contactIds = new Set<Id>();
for(Task t : newTasks) {
if(t.WhoId != null && isContactId(t.WhoId)) {
contactIds.add(t.WhoId);

        }

    }


    Map<Id, Contact> contactMap = retrieveContacts(contactIds);


for(Task t : newTasks) {
if(contactMap.containsKey(t.WhoId)) {
contactMap.get(t.WhoId).No_of_Open_Tasks__c += 1;

        }

    }


    update contactMap.values();

    }
```

```
    public void afterUpdate(List<Task> newTasks, Map< Id, Task> oldTaskMap) {

        Set<Id> contactIds = new Set<Id>();

for(Task t : newTasks) {

if(t.IsClosed && !oldTaskMap.get(t.Id).IsClosed && t.WhoId != null &&
isContactId(t.WhoId)) {

contactIds.add(t.WhoId);

        }

    }


    Map<Id, Contact> contactMap = retrieveContacts(contactIds);


for(Contact con : contactMap.values()) {

con.No_of_Open_Tasks__c = 0;

    }


for(AggregateResult ar : [SELECT WhoId, COUNT(Id) total FROM Task WHERE
IsClosed = false AND WhoId in :contactIds GROUP BY WhoId]) {

        String who = String.valueOf(ar.get('WhoId'));

        Decimal total = (Decimal)(ar.get('total'));

contactMap.get(who).No_of_Open_Tasks__c = total;

    }


    update contactMap.values();

    }


}
```

Our new `retrieveContacts` method simply performs the query in the same way as before but has made the remainder of the code more legible and readable, as well as giving the query a single location to update. I recommend stepping back through this final version of the code to ensure you understand how and why it is an improvemtn on the first version we have seen. The full code is repeated many times in this chapter to show how the code should gradually shift through these small changes to become more readable and easier to work with.

It should be noted that a very strong argument could be made against doing the last change we have made here. For a start, some may argue the improvement in readability is minor and so not worth the extra effort. Additionally, it could be argued that should the query need changing for just the after update context, we would either have to undo this change or update the query and have additional data or a changed query for the after insert context as well.

These are both fair points and come down to personal style and preference. As we are working through an example in a book, I am aiming to show you as many examples of extracting into methods as possible. I would argue that we should also not concern ourselves with if the query changes in the future as we can readily argue *what if the query doesn't change?* As developers, our aims should always be to meet the business requirements as simply and effectively as possible and to leave any code we touch in an equal or better state than how we found it. This last part is the judgment call you will have to make as a developer and so is highlighted here to remind you that there is no perfect code or correct answer in this case, but to work with those around you to determine the optimal for the team.

# Conclusion

In this chapter, we have seen how we can define Apex classes to help us structure our code more effectively and ensure that when we do we do so in the most appropriate manner to encapsulate the functionality. We began by discussing how we define variables for a class and the different access modifiers we can use on these variables. The differences between properties and variables were also discussed and when best to use each.

We then reviewed defining methods within a class for use and how we can use constructors to help us default variables and set our classes upon initialization. We also discussed overloading constructors and methods to provide polymorphism within our code.

Following this, we looked at how we can use the `static` keyword to remove the need for initialization and how it can be combined with the `final` keyword to define constants within our Apex code. We then looked at inner classes and the three main use cases for them with some code examples.

Finally, we wrapped the chapter up with a detailed example of a class where we took our existing trigger code and extracted it into a series of methods within a class to work with. We reviewed the positives and negatives of doing this as well as how we should best make these decisions.

# Questions

1. When should we use an Apex property vs. a variable?
2. What are the four access modifiers for a variable or method?
3. What is the difference between a class running with sharing or without sharing?
4. What does the `static` keyword do to a method?
5. What is the name for providing multiple variations of a constructor or method with different parameters?
6. What are some use cases for inner classes?

# CHAPTER 10

# Apex Class Inheritance

In the last chapter, we discussed how to define and create instances of new Apex classes, including adding variables, methods, and properties. However, as we discussed in *Chapter 2: What is Apex?* Apex is object-oriented meaning classes can inherit from each other and operate in a polymorphic manner. This is what we are going to discuss in this chapter.

## Structure

In this chapter we are going to learn about inheritance and polymorphism using:

- Interfaces
- Abstract classes
- Abstract methods
- Virtual classes
- Virtual methods
- The super keyword

# Objectives

By the end of this chapter you should:

- Be able to define and implement an interface
- Be able to define and extend an abstract class
- Be able to define and extend a virtual class
- Know how to override abstract and virtual methods
- Understand how to use the super keyword

# Interfaces

Interfaces are the most basic form of inheritance within the Apex language and the one developers will most frequently encounter as they implement the Salesforce provided system interfaces in order to run certain asynchronous processes such as Batch Apex.

We can think of an interface as a contract that we are going to agree to implement. Any implementation of this interface must match this agreed contract so that those working with the interface can be confident that a certain set of methods will be available. This can then allow the code to use that interface to utilize different implementations of the interface seamlessly making our code more dynamic and decoupled for resilience.

Let us look at a standard Salesforce example, the `Database.Batchable` interface that Batch Apex classes must implement. Salesforce provides this interface for developers so that they can fulfill the contract specified in the interface and populate the required methods, in this case, `start`, `execute`, and `finish`. We can then request that the Batch Apex job defined by the class be executed and the Salesforce execution engine can perform this task knowing that the required methods will be available. The same execution engine can then be used to run any Batch Apex class in a repeatable and interchangeable fashion.

# Defining an interface

We can define an interface in Apex in a similar manner to defining a class:

```
public interface InterfaceName {


}
```

Where `InterfaceName` is the name we wish to give our interface. When we define an interface, we can provide method signatures, however, the method cannot be implemented. As an example, recall that in *Chapter 2: What is Apex?* We discussed the idea of shapes and using inheritance to allow us to define common methods between these shapes. Let us define a new interface called shape that enables us to retrieve the area for a shape:

```
public interface Shape {

Double getArea();

}
```

Any class that implements this interface must also provide an implementation of this `getArea` method. Note that we do not need to define the accessor for the method, this will be defined by the implementation.

Note to define this interface in our Developer Console, choose to create a new Apex class as before with the name `Shape`, and then replace the class definition with our interface definition and save.

# Implementing an interface

Let us now see how we could implement this newly defined `Shape` interface for a class that represents a rectangle. We first define our class as we would do otherwise:

```
public class Rectangle {


}
```

To implement an interface we add the `implements` keyword followed by the name of the interface that we wish to implement:

```
public class Rectangle implements Shape {


}
```

Finally, we must then implement all of the methods defined in the interface:

```
public class Rectangle implements Shape {

public Double getArea() {

//code goes here
```

```
}
```

```
}
```

In order for us to calculate an area, we are going to need the width and length of our rectangle which we can store as `private` variables and take them in via a constructor. We can then multiply them together to return our rectangle's area:

```
public class Rectangle implements Shape {

private Double length = 0;

private Double width = 0;

public Rectangle(Double l, Double w) {
length = l;
width = w;
    }

public Double getArea() {
return length * width;
        }

}
```

We could repeat this for a `Circle` class as well allowing us to define another shape:

```
public class Circle implements Shape                {

private Double radius = 0;

public Circle(Double r) {
radius = r;
```

```
        }


public Double getArea() {

return Math.PI * radius * radius;

                }


}
```

Now we have 2 implementations of our interface what would it look like to use these interchangeably within our code? If you have not already done so, create open your **Developer Console** and create the Shape interface and the Rectangle and Circle classes implementing the interface as we have just done.

Once this is done, define the following additional class as well:

```
public class PolymorphicShapes {

public static void printArea(Shape s) {

System.debug('The area of our shape is: ' + s.getArea());

}

}
```

Once you have done this, open the execute anonymous window and enter the following code:

```
PolymorphicShapes.printArea(new Rectangle(3,6));

PolymorphicShapes.printArea(new Circle(3));
```

If you execute this code and view the debug logs you should see the debug statements print out the areas of our shapes as we expect. What is important to see here is that our printArea function takes in a Shape instance, that is, an instance of an implementation of our interface. When we call this method, we can pass in instances of either of our shape classes as they both implement the interface. The code within the printArea method knows it has a class instance that implements the Shape interface and can, therefore, call the getArea method with a guarantee it has been implemented.

It should also be noted that a class can implement multiple interfaces, we simply need to list them all after the implements keyword.

# Abstract classes

In the last chapter, we discussed the concept of a utility class that we might implement to define some shared methods for use by a number of classes. This is a good pattern for use when we are considering a set of methods that are external to the underlying structure, for example, may have a utility to retrieve common data and hold it to reduce the number of queries we make. What if instead however we had a method that we wished to define once and share across multiple object instances and multiple types? Similarly, what if we wished to define a common property or member that each instance should use for consistency, an example the `Id` in the `sObject` class.

Looking at the concept of our shapes, we may want to ensure that each shape has a number of properties storing the shape's RGB color values, as well as a method for setting the shape's color to black. We would want these properties and this method to be available on all of our shapes, however, using an interface we can only provide method signatures to implement. For this requirement, we must use an abstract class.

Abstract classes cannot be instantiated themselves, but instead can be extended. An abstract class can have member variables and methods that if they marked as `public` or `protected` can be accessed by the class extending the abstract class.

For our example with shapes, let's define the abstract class that will allow us to manage the colors as discussed above. An `abstract` class is defined as a regular class with the `abstract` keyword before the class name. We can define an `AbstractShape` class as follows:

```
public abstract class AbstractShape {

}
```

We can then define properties for the red, green, and blue values for our colors and a method to set to black as we normally would:

```
public abstract class AbstractShape {

public Integer red;

public Integer green;

public Integer blue;


public void setToBlack() {
red = 0;
```

```
green = 0;

blue = 0;

}

}
```

We can now update our `Rectangle` or `Circle` classes to extend this abstract class by adding extends `AbstractShape` to the end of our class definition but before the `implements` statement:

```
public with sharing class Rectangle extends AbstractShape implements
Shape {

//Existing code

}
```

```
public class Circle extends AbstractShape implements Shape {

//Existing code

}
```

Let's now update our `PolymorphicShapes` class to include a pair of additional methods to test this:

```
public class PolymorphicShapes {

public static void printArea(Shape s) {

System.debug('The area of our shape is: ' + s.getArea());

}

    public static void setColour(AbstractShape s, Integer r, Integer g,
    Integer b) {

s.red = r;

s.green = g;

s.blue = b;

    }
```

```
    public static void makeBlack(AbstractShape s) {

s.setToBlack();

    }

}
```

The new method `setColour` takes in an instance that extends `AbstractShape` (it cannot take in an instance of `AbstractShape` itself as previously discussed) and values for the red, green, and blue channels, setting them accordingly. The `makeBlack` method takes in the `AbstractShape` extension and then calls the `setToBlack` method. After saving all these updates we can then run some execute anonymous code to verify this all works as expected:

```
Rectangle r = new Rectangle(5,5);

Circle c = new Circle(1);

PolymorphicShapes.setColour(r, 123, 33, 78);

System.debug('Rectangle has colour rgb(' + r.red + ',' + r.green + ',' +
r.bluc ı ')');

PolymorphicShapes.makeBlack(c);

System.debug('Circle has colour rgb(' + c.red + ',' + c.green + ',' +
c.blue + ')');
```

If you execute this and view the debug information you should see that the correct color values are printed out for both our rectangle and circle instances.

This is a very powerful feature and allows us to define common methods and properties that we wish to utilize across our classes in a simple way that makes our code easier to manage and maintain (more DRY).

A good question to ask now would be whether we could remove the need for both the interface and the `abstract` class and use just simply an `abstract` class? Is there a method by which we could define just the signature in our `abstract` class for use within our extensions?

# Abstract methods

Abstract methods allow us to meet this exact use case. In the same way that an `abstract` class cannot itself be instantiated, an `abstract` method has no body, only a signature. When providing an implementation, you are overriding the method, telling the system to use your implementation instead.

Let us now update our `AbstractShape` class to include our `getArea` method as an abstract method. To do this, we have to add the `abstract` keyword to the definition of the method as shown below:

```
public abstract class AbstractShape {

public Integer red;

public Integer green;

public Integer blue;


public abstract Double getArea();


public void setToBlack() {

red = 0;

green = 0;

blue = 0;

}

}
```

If we edit our `Circle` class now to remove the interface implementation and try to save the following:

```
public class Circle extends AbstractShape {


private Double radius = 0;


public Circle(Double r) {

radius = r;

}


public Double getArea() {

return Math.PI * radius * radius;
```

```
}
```

```
}
```

We will notice that some errors occur:

- The method must use the override keyword: `Double Circle.getArea()`
- Class `Circle` must implement the abstract method: `Double AbstractShape.getArea()`

Both of these errors are related to the fact that we have defined the body for our class but not told the compiler we are overriding the `abstract` method in the class we are extending. To do this we need to add the `override` keyword to our method definition for `getArea` as shown:

```
public class Circle extends AbstractShape {


private Double radius = 0;


public Circle(Double r) {

radius = r;

}


public override Double getArea() {

return Math.PI * radius * radius;

}

        }

}
```

This code will compile and allow us to work with it. We should make the same updates to the `Rectangle` class:

```
public with sharing class Rectangle extends AbstractShape {


private Double length = 0;
```

```
private Double width = 0;


public Rectangle(Double l, Double w) {

length = l;

width = w;

}


public override Double getArea() {

return length * width;

        }


}
```

And then finally update our `printArea` method from the `PolymorphicShapes` class to use an `AbstractShape` instance rather than a `Shape` instance as we are no longer implementing the interface:

```
public class PolymorphicShapes {

public static void printArea(AbstractShape s) {

System.debug('The area of our shape is: ' + s.getArea());

}


    public static void setColour(AbstractShape s, Integer r, Integer g,
    Integer b) {

s.red = r;

s.green = g;

s.blue = b;

    }


    public static void makeBlack(AbstractShape s) {

s.setToBlack();
```

```
    }

}
```

Finally, let's run our previous execute anonymous statements that we're printing the area to verify this all still works:

```
PolymorphicShapes.printArea(new Rectangle(3,6));

PolymorphicShapes.printArea(new Circle(3));
```

This code executes for us and returns the expected results still.

Abstract methods behave much the same as methods defined in an interface, however, the fact we can define abstract methods and fully implemented concrete methods alongside each other in an abstract class makes them additionally useful when working in situations where both are required.

We have when we want a method defined with no implementation provided, and also a method defined to be inherited with an implementation provided that cannot be changed. What about the case halfway between these, where we wish to provide a default method implementation for our subclasses but still enable them to override this implementation when needed?

# Virtual methods

Virtual methods are the tool in the Apex toolbox that enables us to provide a method with a default implementation that can still be overridden if needed.

Let us look at an example again using our shapes. We can define a virtual method for our shapes that will return an integer for the number of sides for the shape. We will have it return 4 by default as more shapes are quadrilaterals (rectangles, squares, parallelograms, rhombi, etc.) than are triangles, circles, etc.[1]

In our `AbstractShapes` class then we define a `virtual` method `getNumbersOfSides` as follows:

```
public abstract class AbstractShape {

public Integer red;

public Integer green;

public Integer blue;
```

---

[1] We will see a more concrete Salesforce oriented example later, however for the purposes of demonstration I want to continue using our shapes to see how these concepts interact together.

```
public abstract Double getArea();


public virtual Integer getNumberOfSides() {

return 4;

}


public void setToBlack() {

red = 0;

green = 0;

blue = 0;

}

}
```

In our Circle class, we will want to override this and instead return 1. We can do this in the same way we overrode our abstract method previously:

```
public class Circle extends AbstractShape {


private Double radius = 0;


public Circle(Double r) {

radius = r;

}


public override Double getArea() {

return Math.PI * radius * radius;

}
```

```
public override Integer getNumberOfSides() {

return 1;

}


}
```

In our **Execute Anonymous** window, if we then execute the following Apex:

```
Rectangle r = new Rectangle(5,5);

Circle c = new Circle(1);

System.debug('A rectangle has ' + r.getNumberOfSides() + ' sides');

System.debug('A circle has ' + c.getNumberOfSides() + ' side');
```

The our debug logs will print out A rectangle has 4 sides and A circle has 1 side as we expect.

Virtual methods are extremely useful in allowing you as a developer to provide a default implementation for a method that subclasses and extensions can utilize without the need to reimplement each time, whilst enabling the subclass to override as required. We will see at the end of this chapter how this can be extremely useful in a trigger handler class like the class we defined in the previous chapter to add additional flexibility and functionality.

Before we do this though, we need to review the final tool in our inheritance toolbox, virtual classes.

# Virtual classes

A virtual class is very much like an abstract class in that it can be extended by other classes and contain virtual methods that can be overridden by the subclass. Unlike abstract classes, virtual classes cannot contain abstract methods but can be instantiated. This means that we can use a virtual class to provide a complete default implementation and then extend the class and override the methods as needed.

To define a virtual class, simply use the virtual keyword as part of the class definition:

```
public virtual class MyVirtualClass {

//virtual or concrete methods and member variables
```

}

Any class that is then going to extend our `virtual` class then uses the `extends` keyword in its definition:

```
public class MyClassExtension extends MyVirtualClass {

//can use all concreate member variables and methods from MyVirtualClass

//can override all virtual methods from MyVirtualClass

}
```

Let's see a more detailed example of a `virtual` class in an updated trigger handler.

# Updated trigger handler

In the last chapter, we abstracted away the code that was in our `TaskTrigger` into an Apex class called `TaskTriggerHandler` as follows:

```
public without sharing class TaskTriggerHandler {


private static final String KEY_PREFIX = Contact.sObjectType.getDescribe().
getKeyPrefix();


private Boolean isContactId(Id recordId) {

return String.valueOf(recordId).startsWith(KEY_PREFIX);

}


private Map<Id, Contact> retrieveContacts(Set<Id> contactIds) {

return new Map<Id, Contact>([SELECT Id, No_of_Open_Tasks__c FROM Contact
WHERE Id in :contactIds]);

}


public void afterInsert(List<Task> newTasks) {

Set<Id> contactIds = new Set<Id>();
```

```
for(Task t : newTasks) {

if(t.WhoId != null && isContactId(t.WhoId)) {

contactIds.add(t.WhoId);

}

    }


    Map<Id, Contact> contactMap = retrieveContacts(contactIds);


for(Task t : newTasks) {

if(contactMap.containsKey(t.WhoId)) {

contactMap.get(t.WhoId).No_of_Open_Tasks__c += 1;

        }

}


update contactMap.values();

}


public void afterUpdate(List<Task> newTasks, Map<Id, Task> oldTaskMap) {

Set<Id> contactIds = new Set<Id>();

for(Task t : newTasks) {

if(t.IsClosed && !oldTaskMap.get(t.Id).IsClosed && t.WhoId != null &&
isContactId(t.WhoId)) {

contactIds.add(t.WhoId);

}

}


    Map<Id, Contact> contactMap = retrieveContacts(contactIds);
```

```
for(Contact con : contactMap.values()) {

con.No_of_Open_Tasks__c = 0;

}


for(AggregateResult ar : [SELECT WhoId, COUNT(Id) total FROM Task WHERE
IsClosed = false AND WhoId in :contactIds GROUP BY WhoId]) {

String who = String.valueOf(ar.get('WhoId'));

    Decimal total = (Decimal)(ar.get('total'));

contactMap.get(who).No_of_Open_Tasks__c = total;

}


update contactMap.values();

    }


}
```

In our `TaskTrigger` we also had the following code:

```
trigger TaskTrigger on Task (after insert, after update) {

    switch on Trigger.operationType {

        when AFTER_INSERT {

TaskTriggerHandler handler = new TaskTriggerHandler();

handler.afterInsert((List<Task>)Trigger.new);

        }

        when AFTER_UPDATE {

TaskTriggerHandler handler = new TaskTriggerHandler();

handler.afterUpdate((List<Task>)Trigger.new,   (Map<Id,   Task>)Trigger.
oldMap);

        }
```

```
    }

}
```

For each trigger we write, we are going to want to perform a lot of the same operations:

- Determine which trigger context we are running in
- Execute the correct method for that context

We do not want to have to redefine this code multiple times and so it is an ideal candidate for an inheritance to be used. The first question, however, is do we want an `interface`, an `abstract` class, or a `virtual` class?

We have already noted that we want the code to be reusable and provide some of the functionality for repeated use so that rules out an `interface` as in an `interface` there are no method implementations, only signatures.

From this, we also know that we will not want `abstract` methods, again wanting methods with full signatures leaving us the choice of an `abstract` class with only concrete and `virtual` methods, or a `virtual` class.

We know that `abstract` classes cannot be instantiated and therefore cannot have tests written for them without full implementation. We are going to cover testing in detail in the next chapter, but it is important to note that one of the key differences from an Apex developer's perspective between a `virtual` and an `abstract` class is the ability to test them in isolation from any extensions. Therefore for our use case, we are going to define a `virtual` class.

Let us start by defining our `virtual TriggerHandler` class:

```
public virtual class TriggerHandler {


}
```

Firstly, let us define default methods for all of our trigger contexts. We can then let each extension of this class `override` this implementation whilst still providing a default. For this we will create a series of `virtual` methods for each of our possible trigger contexts:

```
public virtual class TriggerHandler {

public virtual void beforeInsert(){}

public virtual void beforeUpdate(){}

public virtual void beforeDelete(){}
```

```
public virtual void afterInsert(){}

public virtual void afterUpdate(){}

public virtual void afterDelete(){}

public virtual void afterUndelete(){}

}
```

These methods are all empty as by default we do not want our trigger implementation to make any changes it does not need to.

Let's update our TaskTriggerHandler extend this class:

```
public without sharing class TaskTriggerHandler extends TriggerHandler {


private static final String KEY_PREFIX = Contact.sObjectType.getDescribe().
getKeyPrefix();


private Boolean isContactId(Id recordId) {

return String.valueOf(recordId).startsWith(KEY_PREFIX);

    }


private Map<Id, Contact> retrieveContacts(Set<Id> contactIds) {

return new Map<Id, Contact>([SELECT Id, No_of_Open_Tasks__c FROM Contact
WHERE Id in :contactIds]);

}


public override void afterInsert() {

Set<Id> contactIds = new Set<Id>();

for(Task t : (List<Task>)Trigger.new) {

if(t.WhoId != null && isContactId(t.WhoId)) {

contactIds.add(t.WhoId);

}
```

```
        }


    Map<Id, Contact> contactMap = retrieveContacts(contactIds);


for(Task t : (List<Task>)Trigger.new) {
if(contactMap.containsKey(t.WhoId)) {
contactMap.get(t.WhoId).No_of_Open_Tasks__c += 1;
        }
}


update contactMap.values();
}


public override void afterUpdate() {
Set<Id> contactIds = new Set<Id>();
for(Task t : (List<Task>)Trigger.new) {
        Task oldTask = (Task)(Trigger.oldMap.get(t.Id));
=if(t.IsClosed && !oldTask.IsClosed && t.WhoId != null && isContactId(t.
WhoId)) {
contactIds.add(t.WhoId);
}
}


    Map<Id, Contact> contactMap = retrieveContacts(contactIds);


for(Contact con : contactMap.values()) {
con.No_of_Open_Tasks__c = 0;
```

```
}
```

```
for(AggregateResult ar : [SELECT WhoId, COUNT(Id) total FROM Task WHERE
IsClosed = false AND WhoId in :contactIds GROUP BY WhoId]) {

String who = String.valueOf(ar.get('WhoId'));

    Decimal total = (Decimal)(ar.get('total'));

contactMap.get(who).No_of_Open_Tasks__c = total;

}
```

```
update contactMap.values();

}
```

```
}
```

We have marked both of the methods as overriding the default ones from our implementation and have reverted to using the trigger context variables for retrieving our data.

We can now update our TaskTrigger to the following:

```
trigger TaskTrigger on Task (after insert, after update) {

    switch on Trigger.operationType {

    when AFTER_INSERT {

TaskTriggerHandler handler = new TaskTriggerHandler();

handler.afterInsert();

        }

        when AFTER_UPDATE {

TaskTriggerHandler handler = new TaskTriggerHandler();

handler.afterUpdate();

        }

    }
```

```
}
```

This has abstracted away from the need for us to pass in the correct data to the method, each method knows what data it needs from the context. However, we still have logic running in our trigger that is likely to be run elsewhere in selecting the correct method to run. Let's update the `TriggerHandler` to resolve this.

To our `TriggerHandler` we are going to add a new method called run that will be a concrete implementation which determines which context we are in and which method from the trigger we should run. Firstly, we can add the method signature:

```
public virtual class TriggerHandler {

public virtual void beforeInsert(){}

public virtual void beforeUpdate(){}

public virtual void beforeDelete(){}

public virtual void afterInsert(){}

public virtual void afterUpdate(){}

public virtual void afterDelete(){}

public virtual void afterUndelete(){}


public void run() {


}


}
```

We want our method to determine which context we are in and then run the correct method. We can use the `switch` statement in our existing `TaskTrigger` as the basis for our method to start with:

```
public virtual class TriggerHandler {

public virtual void beforeInsert(){}

public virtual void beforeUpdate(){}

public virtual void beforeDelete(){}

public virtual void afterInsert(){}
```

```
public virtual void afterUpdate(){}

public virtual void afterDelete(){}

public virtual void afterUndelete(){}


public void run() {

switch on Trigger.operationType {

    when AFTER_INSERT {

this.afterInsert();

}

    when AFTER_UPDATE {

this.afterUpdate();

}

  }

        }


}
```

A few things to note. Firstly we are using this keyword here to ensure that the execution calls the correct method for the current instance and not the instance of the parent class (i.e. calls the overridden method if it exists and not always the default). Secondly, our methods for the different contexts are still marked as public even though we do not intend on calling them except via our run method. As a next step let us mark them as protected so that they are visible to the TriggerHandler and it's subclasses and extensions, but not to other code. We can also extend our switch statement to handle the other trigger contexts:

```
public virtual class TriggerHandler {

protected virtual void beforeInsert(){}

protected virtual void beforeUpdate(){}

protected virtual void beforeDelete(){}

protected virtual void afterInsert(){}
```

```
protected virtual void afterUpdate(){}

protected virtual void afterDelete(){}

protected virtual void afterUndelete(){}


public void run() {

switch on Trigger.operationType {

      when BEFORE_INSERT {

this.beforeInsert();

}

      when AFTER_INSERT {

this.afterInsert();

}

      when BEFORE_UPDATE {

this.beforeUpdate();

}

      when AFTER_UPDATE {

this.afterUpdate();

}

      when BEFORE_DELETE {

this.beforeDelete();

}

      when AFTER_DELETE {

this.afterDelete();

}

      when AFTER_UNDELETE {

this.afterUndelete();

}
```

```
    }
}
```

```
}
```

We should update the signatures in our `TaskTriggerHandler` to be protected:

```
public without sharing class TaskTriggerHandler extends TriggerHandler {
```

```
protected override void afterInsert() {

//Previous code remains

}
```

```
protected override void afterUpdate() {

//Previous code remains

}
```

```
}
```

Finally, we can simplify our `TaskTrigger` code dramatically:

```
trigger TaskTrigger on Task (after insert, after update) {

TaskTriggerHandler handler = new TaskTriggerHandler();

handler.run();

}
```

This trigger code is much cleaner and abstracts away all logic from our triggers in a simple and repeatable fashion. It highlights a good use case for `virtual` classes and methods to make code more reusable and easier to work with.

# The super keyword

The final thing for us to understand in this chapter is the `super` keyword. When working with virtual classes we are able to define constructors:

```
public virtual class VirtualExample {

    public VirtualExample() {

        this('default');

    }


    public VirtualExample(String s) {

System.debug(s);

    }


public void printHello() {

System.debug('Hello');

}

}
```

This example class has 2 constructors that will print code out to the debug logs. If we were to define an extension to this, we can use the super keyword to access methods from the class we are extending or to call the constructors from the parent class.

```
public class VirtualExtensionExample extends VirtualExample{

    public VirtualExtensionExample() {

        //call parent constructor

super();

    }


public VirtualExtensionExample(String s) {

        //call parent constructor

        super(s);

    }
```

```
  public void hi() {

//call parent method

super.printHello();

  }

}
```

If we execute the following anonymous code:

```
VirtualExtensionExample example = new VirtualExtensionExample();

example.hi();
```

Then inspecting the debug logs will show that the methods from our parent class `VirtualExample` have been called. Developers should be aware of the `super` keyword when working with `abstract` or `virtual` classes to enable them to call methods on the parent class, and in the case of `virtual` classes, constructors where appropriate.

# Conclusion

In this chapter, we have covered off the features within Apex that make it a fully-featured object-oriented language. This chapter is probably one of the more difficult chapters to fully understand as a lot of the material is quite abstract. Do not fear, as a new developer you should first of all focus on building working solutions and then look to see how you can best use the features we have covered to improve your code. For a lot of developers and projects, you will not need to work with these concepts for a while, and so can always revisit this material again when appropriate. In many situations, you won't look at extending a class or implementing an interface until you do so for one of the system classes or interfaces when working with a tool like Batch Apex. In *Chapter 12: Callouts in Apex*, we are going to see a concrete example of implementing an interface when working on testing web service callouts. Before we get into testing web service callouts, we first have to start in *Chapter 11: Testing Apex* and understand how to test our Apex in general.

# Questions

1. What is the difference between an interface, an `abstract` class, and a `virtual` class?
2. What types of methods can be defined in an `abstract` class?
3. Can we instantiate an `abstract` class?
4. What types of methods can be defined in a `virtual` class?

# CHAPTER 11
# Testing Apex

In *Chapter 2. What is Apex?* we highlighted the fact that in order to deploy Apex to a production environment we must have achieved 75% code coverage from our unit tests. Salesforce demands this for all code deployed to production to ensure that developers, and in particular those developing products for the AppExchange, have verified that their code works as expected. In this chapter, we are going to cover off testing in Apex and how to test your Apex code properly.

## Structure

In this chapter we are going to learn:

- What is unit testing?
- What code coverage is and how it is calculated
- How we define a unit test in Apex
- How we run a unit test in Apex
- Exceptions and exception handling
- How to create test data

# Objectives

By the end of this chapter you should:

- Be able to define and run a unit test in Apex
- Be able to define custom exceptions
- Know how to throw and catch exceptions
- Know how to test for exceptions
- Understand how to create test data in a repeatable manner

# What is unit testing?

Let us start by discussing what a test is within the context of Apex and more formally what is meant by unit testing. When we write code, we are building up a system made of a number of individual building blocks that together perform some function. Typically, each of these building blocks is an Apex method within our solution, and these many method calls are chained together in order to define a more detailed process. Each of these methods or individual blocks of code that are run is referred to as a unit of code:

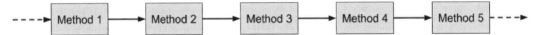

*Figure 11.1: A process is made up of many methods chained together.*
*Each method is a unit of code in the process.*

When developing, we want to ensure that our code is easy to work with and maintain, and that each unit of code operates correctly without unintended side effects. In an ideal system, each method should be well defined and encapsulated so that the internal operations of the method do not matter and if required we can alter the code inside each method without impacting the rest of the system, provided the input and output remain the same.

For example, in *Chapter 9: Apex Classes* we constructed the following Calculator class:

```
public with sharing class Calculator        {



public static Integer add(Integer item1, Integer item2) {

if(item1 == null || item2 == null) {

return 0;
```

```
}

return item1 + item2;

        }


}
```

When working with the add method, it is largely irrelevant to the overall process of how exactly the values are summed, only that they return the correct value. If we wanted to change the implementation of the add method to:

```
public static Integer add(Integer item1, Integer item2) {

if(item1 == null || item2 == null) {

return 0;

}

for(Integer i = 0; i < item2; i++) {

item1++;

}

return item1;

}
```

Or even:

```
public static Integer add(Integer item1, Integer item2) {

if(item1 == null || item2 == null) {

return 0;

        }


return ((-1 * item1) - item2) * -1;

}
```

All three methods should give the same result, the only difference being that the way in which the method performs the task is either simpler or more convoluted. To the end-user and the remainder of the process, the internal workings of the unit do not matter, only that we obtain the correct result.

Unit testing in development is then the process of testing a unit of code within a process to ensure that it behaves as expected. By writing a code-based unit test, we can have a quick and repeatable way of running a series of tests against our code that will inform us of whether the code operated as expected. In our examples above, we could have a series of tests that verify the outcome of the add method is correct and enable us to use these differing implementations without any impact on the overall process.

# Code coverage

What is meant then by code coverage? Recall we have stated multiple times that code coverage must be greater than or equal to 75% to allow us to deploy code to a production environment[1]. How is this value calculated?

Whenever we run a unit test, the code we are testing (and any other code run as part of the setup or testing process) will be executed. Within each class and trigger, Salesforce will store which lines are executed by unit tests and which lines are not. Those lines that are executed are marked as *covered*, those lines that are not executed are marked as *not covered*. The code coverage is then calculated as:

*Code coverage = number of covered lines / (number of covered + number of not covered lines)*

Additionally, certain rules are in place around what lines are counted as available for coverage. The following lines are not considered for code coverage:

- Comments
- Blank lines
- Partial statements on a line (e.g. a SOQL Query written over 2 lines is considered as 1 line)
- System.debug() statements
- Curly braces { }

If you have multiple statements on a single line, for example if we had the code snippet:

```
[String x = 'Test'; Integer i = 0; i++;]
```

then this is counted as a single line. Finally, for conditional branches, only executed conditions are credited for coverage. This means that for an `if-else` statement both the `if` and the `else` branches must be tested independently.

---

1  More precisely, the total coverage across all Apex code must be 75% and each Apex trigger must have some coverage.

As a best practice, a developer should always aim to 100% cover their code to ensure that it operates as expected. In my experience, testing is an undervalued part of the process for many developers and is often left to the end of their work and treated as an afterthought. Testing should be a key part of any development work you are doing as it enables you to have confidence that the code you have written operates in the expected manner and allows you to catch any bugs early before they reach users. For this reason, it is common to include the code achieving over 85% coverage and all tests passing as part of a team's definition of done for work.

# Defining a Unit Test

Let us write a very basic test for our `Calculator` class to start with. We begin by defining a new Apex class to hold our tests. A common naming convention is to name the test class for an Apex class as `ClassName_Test` as this will ensure that classes and their corresponding tests are grouped correctly within any IDEs or lists. For our `Calculator` class then, the test class will be called `Calculator_Test`. We define a test class in a similar way to how we define a regular class:

```
@isTest

private with sharing class Calculator_Test {



}
```

There are however two notable differences in our definition.

Firstly the class starts with the `@isTest` annotation. This annotation tells Salesforce to ignore this class when both calculating the overall code coverage for the org and when calculating the overall usage of Apex throughout the Org (there is a 6MB limit of Apex code for the organization).

Secondly, we have defined the class as `private` rather than `public` as we had seen previously. The reason for this is that we do not want this class or its methods to be available to any other code, it should only ever be executed by the test runner. Marking the class as `private` will ensure this happens.

Apart from these 2 features, our class definition is much the same as any other Apex class and this is done on purpose. Rather than requiring you to learn a new framework or toolkit for testing, Salesforce has made writing tests as close to writing other Apex code as possible.

Each test class we define will have a series of test methods. Test methods are defined in the following way:

- Annotated by `@isTest`
- Must be `private`
- Must be `static`
- Must have a `void` return type, that is the method returns no data
- Must take in no parameters

These requirements ensure that the test methods can be run independently of one another and do not leak data into the system. If we wanted to define a test for our add method with 2 positive integers we could do so as:

```
@isTest

private with sharing class Calculator_Test        {


@isTest

private static void testTwoPositiveIntegers() {


}
}
```

This is our first test method defined. It does not test much currently, but before we start adding in more code I would like to briefly discuss what happens in a test.

# What happens in a test?

Broadly speaking, I think of a test as being composed of 3 steps:

1. Setting up of data required for the test to run
2. Execute the code under test to perform an action
3. Assert that the action has had the intended consequences.

For the majority of developers, steps 1 and 2 are self-evident, you cannot run some code without the data required and you cannot test some code without running it. However, many developers in the Salesforce ecosystem fail to properly perform step 3 and assert on some data. Why is this?

Earlier we discussed how Salesforce requires you to have 75% coverage across your code in order to deploy to a production environment. As we also discussed, for code to be covered merely means that it has been executed by one of our tests. It does not require that the test include an assertion on the outcome. This has lead to many developers writing tests that do not actually assert on an outcome but merely execute the code.

This is a dangerous precedent to set and leaves your code vulnerable to undiscovered bugs. You should ensure that all tests you write have at least one assertion in them to verify that the code being tested has acted in the manner expected. If you do not do so then you have no guarantee that it is working.

By properly writing tests that include assertions you will find a multitude of bugs early and be able to fix them before users find them. I would almost guarantee that every time I write a test class for some code I have worked on I find at least one bug or edge case that I or someone else has not thought about. It may even be a new requirement that nobody in the business has discussed fully, but by finding it early and often you can ensure that it is handled appropriately. It will also enable you to confidently state that your code does meet the requirements laid out with verifiable evidence.

# Writing our test

Now that we know what we should have in our test, let us begin populating our testTwoPositiveIntegers method. Following our 3 steps above, we will want to create some test data (in this case it is just having 2 positive integers), then execute the code we want to test (that is call our add method), and then finally assert we get the right value back. In code this will look like the following:

```
@isTest

private with sharing class Calculator_Test {


@isTest

private static void testTwoPositiveIntegers() {

//Setup our test data

Integer x = 5;

Integer y = 9;


//Execute the method we wish to test

Integer result = Calculator.add(x, y);
```

```
//Assert we get the correct result

System.assertEquals(14, result, 'Incorrect result returned from add
method');

}

}
```

Setting up our test data and calling the method utilizes Apex features we have seen before, but the final step has a new method we have not encountered yet, `System.assertEquals`.

Salesforce has provided 3 assertion methods that can be used within a test context to enable developers to validate their tests are running correctly, they are:

- `System.assert(Boolean testValue, String failureMessage)`: This method takes in a `Boolean` value and will fail if that `Boolean` is `false` returning the `failureMessage`

- `System.assertEquals(expectedValue, actualValue, String failureMessage)`: This method compares the `expectedValue` and `actualValue` and will fail if they are not equal, returning the `failureMessage`

- `System.assertNotEquals(expectedValue, actualValue, String failureMessage)`: This method compares the `expectedValue` and `actualValue` and will fail if they are equal, returning the `failureMessage`

It is important to note here that when we say "returning the `failureMessage`", we mean throwing an exception that cannot be handled and displaying that message through the test runner. When we run the tests that are in our test class, should one of the assertions fail, the system will throw an exception that cannot be caught or handled and display the failure message if one is provided. Note that the `failureMessage` parameter in all three methods is optional, but it is a best practice to include one for debugging purposes.

In our test we have utilized `System.assertEquals` to validate that the data we get back from the add method is correct and have provided an appropriate error message should this have failed. To run this in the **Developer Console** press the **Run Test** button at the top right of any test class to run just that test (marked as 1 in *Figure 11.2* below), or choose **Test** then **New Run** from the menu bar to choose tests to run. You can see a breakdown of test results using the test tab (marked as 2 in *Figure 11.2*) and a view of the code coverage in the **Code Coverage** window (marked as 3 in *Figure 11.2*):

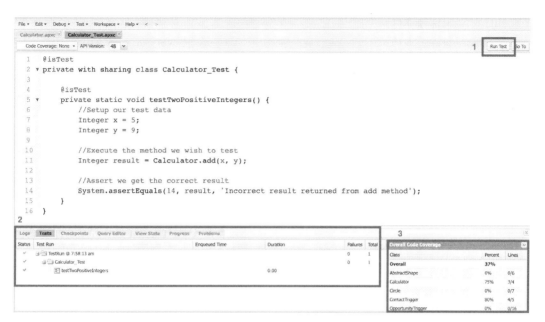

*Figure 11.2:* Running tests and viewing results in the Developer Console

If you double click on a class listed in the **Code Coverage** window the Developer
Console will open the class and highlight the lines that are covered in blue and are
not covered in red to help you visualize the additional paths that need testing. As
shown in *Figure 11.3* below, line 5 is not currently covered and so we would need to
add another test to cover this code path:

*Figure 11.3:* Viewing a class' code coverage.

# Exception handling and testing exceptions

So far we have not discussed what to do in our code when something goes bad. Exceptions and exception handling are an integral part of our development and need to be handled appropriately. So far by virtue of the nature of the examples we have produced we have coded defensively to avoid errors, but let us now start introducing them into the system to correctly handle them.

## Standard exceptions

There are a variety of standard exceptions that Salesforce will throw if we do something wrong. A good example is the (infamous) `NullPointerException`. When coding in Salesforce you can wrap code in a `try-catch` block to handle exceptions more gracefully and allow your code to continue or end. The format for a `try-catch` block is:

```
try {

//Perform some code that may fail

} catch(Exception ex) {

//Handle exception appropriately

}
```

You can catch the generic `Exception` class like we have done in the code snippet above, catch a specific type of exception, or have multiple `catch` blocks for different error types:

```
try {

//Run code

} catch(DMLException dx) {

System.debug('DML Exception: ' + dx.getMessage());

} catch(NullPointerException nx) {

System.debug('Null Pointer Exception: ' + nx.getMessage());

}
```

# Custom exceptions

The generic `Exception` class can also be extended to create custom exception classes that can help in improving debugging and feedback to the user:

```
public class CalculatorException extends Exception {


}
```

This is the most basic extension in order to create a custom exception and allows us to throw our exceptions as required to improve our debugging. We can now create new exceptions and throw them by using:

```
throw new CalculatorException('My error message');
```

How do we test this in Apex? If you have not yet added the `Calculator`, `Calculator_Test` and `CalculatorException` classes to your environment, do so now and update the `Calculator` as follows:

```
public with sharing class Calculator {


public static Integer add(Integer item1, Integer item2) {

if(item1 == null || item2 == null) {

throw new CalculatorException('You cannot use null as a parameter');

}

return item1 + item2;

}


}
```

Now if someone passes in `null` as a value for our add method a custom `CalculatorException` will be thrown that gives an error message as shown above.

In order to test this, we need to verify 2 things:

1. Verify that the code did not execute and did throw an error.
2. Verify that the error message was returned as expected.

Let's write a new test for this. Firstly we want to define our test as before but this time pass in a null value for either item1 or item2[2]:

```
@isTest

private static void testNullItemException() {

//Setup our test data

Integer x = null;

Integer y = 9;


//Execute the method we wish to test

Integer result = Calculator.add(x, y);

}
```

We expect this to error when we call add so we should firstly wrap the method in a try-catch block to catch our CalculatorException:

```
@isTest

private static void testNullItemException() {

//Setup our test data

Integer x = null;

Integer y = 9;


//Execute the method we wish to test

try {

Integer result = Calculator.add(x, y);

} catch(CalculatorException ex) {


}

}
```

---

2    In a full test class we would test item1 being null and item2 being valid, item2 being null and item1 being valid, both being null and both being valid to ensure we have covered all potential cases.

We then said we needed to verify 2 things. Firstly, we wanted to check that our code did not execute, i.e. that an error was thrown. If no error is thrown by our `add` method then the code will continue to execute the next line. As the next line is the `catch` block the code will pass the `catch` block and just end the method. This will look like our test is passing when in fact it is not. So how do we show an error here?

The answer is to use a `System.assert` method, but to pass in a hardcoded `false` value. This will always throw an error if executed and we can return a message to state that an exception should have been thrown. If we add this our code now looks like:

```
@isTest

private static void testNullItemException() {

//Setup our test data

Integer x = null;

Integer y = 9;


//Execute the method we wish to test

try {

Integer result = Calculator.add(x, y);

System.assert(false, 'An exception should have occurred and did not.');

} catch(CalculatorException ex) {


}
}
```

Finally, then, we need to verify that the error message we expect was returned. This we can do in the `catch` block using the `System.assertEquals` method on the message the exception returns:

```
@isTest

private static void testNullItemException() {

//Setup our test data

Integer x = null;
```

```
Integer y = 9;


//Execute the method we wish to test

try {

Integer result = Calculator.add(x, y);

System.assert(false, 'An exception should have occurred and did not.');

} catch(CalculatorException ex) {

System.assertEquals('You cannot use null as a parameter', ex.getMessage(),
'Incorrect exception message returned.');

}

}
```

If we run this test against our updated `Calculator` class it will pass and we will have improved our system testing to cover negative as well as positive code paths.

# Creating test data

As described above, the first step in our test should be creating our test data. Sometimes we will need to insert different records into the database as part of this data setup in order to allow us to perform the actions we want to undertake. One of the attributes we want for our test classes and methods is for them to be fast to run and execute. This will make it much simpler for us to deploy as well as ensure that we can run them regularly as a developer to check the status of our code.

In the past few chapters, we have been building out our `TaskTriggerHandler` class and finished the last chapter with the following code for the `afterInsert` method:

```
public override void afterInsert() {

Set<Id> contactIds = new Set<Id>();

for(Task t : (List<Task>)Trigger.new) {

if(t.WhoId != null && isContactId(t.WhoId)) {

contactIds.add(t.WhoId);

}

}
```

```
    Map<Id, Contact> contactMap = retrieveContacts(contactIds);


for(Task t : (List<Task>)Trigger.new) {

if(contactMap.containsKey(t.WhoId)) {

contactMap.get(t.WhoId).No_of_Open_Tasks__c += 1;

    }

}


update contactMap.values();

}
```

In order for us to test this code, we will need to insert some task records to fire the trigger and have a contact record available to associate the record with.

Let us start by defining a new test class `TaskTriggerHandler_Test` and declaring a test method for our first test where we will validate that the `No_of_Open_Tasks__c` field is incremented correctly:

```
@isTest

private with sharing class TaskTriggerHandler_Test {


@isTest

private static void testIncrementOnNewTask() {


//Create our test data

Contact con = new Contact();

con.FirstName = 'Marco';

con.LastName = 'Polo';

con.Phone = '111111111';

insert con;
```

```
Task t = new Task();

t.WhoId = con.Id;

t.Subject = 'Test task';


//Execute the code we want to test

insert t;


//We need to retrieve the Contact record again to check the value has
been updated

con = [SELECT No_of_Open_Tasks__c FROM Contact WHERE Id = :con.Id];

System.assertEquals(1, con.No_of_Open_Tasks__c, 'Incorrect number of open
tasks set on contact');

    }

}
```

If we save and run this test it should pass. In this test, we have done a few different things which we should discuss.

Firstly, when creating our contact, note we have had to provide a phone number otherwise our contact trigger would have thrown an exception for us. This is the code we created originally and highlights that we should be aware when adding such validation of unintended consequences. If we had added that check to an existing code base, potentially all our existing tests would fail and need updating.

Secondly, the code we want to test is just the insert call on the task record as that is the statement that will cause our trigger to fire and run.

Finally, once this has happened we query for the contact again using its Id to ensure we get the exact record match before asserting on the value.

Salesforce has also ensured that no data leaks out from our tests by automatically segregating it. Any data created or changed during the execution of a test is rolled back and removed after the test has run. This helps us separate our tests from our production code and keeps the data in our environment clean.

This is a real-world scenario with real-world test code and highlights how we can go about creating test data for use within the test class. Let us now create a basic test for the afterUpdate method:

```
protected override void afterUpdate() {

Set<Id> contactIds = new Set<Id>();

for(Task t : (List<Task>)Trigger.new) {

    Task oldTask = (Task)(Trigger.oldMap.get(t.Id));

if(t.IsClosed && !oldTask.IsClosed && t.WhoId != null && isContactId(t.
WhoId)) {

contactIds.add(t.WhoId);

}

}


    Map<Id, Contact> contactMap = retrieveContacts(contactIds);


for(Contact con : contactMap.values()) {

con.No_of_Open_Tasks__c = 0;

}


for(AggregateResult ar : [SELECT WhoId, COUNT(Id) total FROM Task WHERE
IsClosed = false AND WhoId in :contactIds GROUP BY WhoId]) {

        String who = String.valueOf(ar.get('WhoId'));

        Decimal total = (Decimal)(ar.get('total'));

contactMap.get(who).No_of_Open_Tasks__c = total;

}


update contactMap.values();

}
```

We would need to create a contact record again, assign a new task to the contact, check the value is correct, mark the task as complete, and then re-evaluate the total. The code to do this would be similar to our first test:

```
@isTest

private static void testDecrementOnClosedTask() {


    //Create our test data

    Contact con = new Contact();

    con.FirstName = 'Marco';

    con.LastName = 'Polo';

    con.Phone = '111111111';

    insert con;


    Task t = new Task();

    t.WhoId = con.Id;

    t.Subject = 'Test task';

    insert t;


    //Let us verify our data is setup correctly

    con = [SELECT No_of_Open_Tasks__c FROM Contact WHERE Id = :con.Id];

    System.assertEquals(1, con.No_of_Open_Tasks__c, 'Incorrect number of open
    tasks set on contact');


    //Now update the task status and commit the change

    t.Status = 'Completed';

    update t;


    con = [SELECT No_of_Open_Tasks__c FROM Contact WHERE Id = :con.Id];

    System.assertEquals(0, con.No_of_Open_Tasks__c, 'Incorrect number of open
    tasks set on contact');

}
```

This test when saved will also execute as expected and pass. Because we are doing an update, note that I have included verification of our state before performing the test we wish to undertake by checking the `No_of_Open_Tasks__c` is set to 1. This is not required, and different developers will debate whether this should be included or not. Personally, I do so to ensure the integrity of my data before and after the test where it will be expected to have a value set by code, and also to help make any errors I receive more granular should the tests fail. If this test fails on the second assertion, I know the issue is in the `afterUpdate`. If it fails on the first assertion, I know it will be in the `afterInsert` and would expect my other test to fail. It is in the edge cases where this does not happen because of a declarative process or flow that this debugging can become more difficult and this extra layer of detail can assist.

# Using @TestSetup

One of the principles we have encountered a number of times throughout the book is that of being DRY in our coding and not repeating things. This same principle should also be applied to our testing. In our 2 tests, we have repeated the creation of our contact record. Whenever we call a DML statement within our tests all of the save order of execution will occur. This can dramatically slow down the speed of our tests if we are doing multiple insertions or updates as part of the test setup, and when running a number of tests at once can severely slow development time down.

Similarly, consider the fact that we have got some code in our contact creation to ensure we have a phone number as we know this is a requirement from our other trigger. What would happen if another field on the contact was made required by an administrator or developer? Our tests would then fail as they did not meet these criteria and the contact creation code would need updating in every place we had it.

In order to combat dealing with these issues, we should extract our contact creation code into a single reusable method. Within a test, we have a special annotation we can use called `@TestSetup` that will mark a method to be executed before the start of any of the tests within that class. This method can be used to perform test data setup once. Each test can then alter the data as needed as part of the test, and following the execution of the test, the data is returned to its original state.

Let us now extract the creation of the contact record into an `@TestSetup` annotated method. Firstly we should define our method and annotate it with `@TestSetup`:

```
@TestSetup

private static void setupData() {

Contact con = new Contact();
```

```
con.FirstName = 'Marco';

con.LastName = 'Polo';

con.Phone = '111111111';

insert con;

}
```

This code will then run when our test class is loaded and make this data available to both tests. We now need to refactor these tests to retrieve the needed data instead of creating it as follows:

```
@isTest

private with sharing class TaskTriggerHandler_Test {


    @TestSetup

    private static void setupData() {

        Contact con = new Contact();

con.FirstName = 'Marco';

con.LastName = 'Polo';

con.Phone = '111111111';

        insert con;

    }


@isTest

private static void testIncrementOnNewTask() {


//Create our test data

Contact con = [SELECT Id FROM Contact LIMIT 1];


Task t = new Task();
```

```
t.WhoId = con.Id;

t.Subject = 'Test task';


//Execute the code we want to test

insert t;


//We need to retrieve the Contact record again to check the value has
been updated

con = [SELECT No_of_Open_Tasks__c FROM Contact WHERE Id = :con.Id];

System.assertEquals(1, con.No_of_Open_Tasks__c, 'Incoprrect number of
open tasks set on contact');

}


    @isTest
    private static void testDecrementOnClosedTask() {


        //Create our test data
        Contact con = [SELECT Id FROM Contact LIMIT 1];


        Task t = new Task();
t.WhoId = con.Id;
t.Subject = 'Test task';
        insert t;


        //Let us verify our data is setup correctly
        con = [SELECT No_of_Open_Tasks__c FROM Contact WHERE Id = :con.Id];
System.assertEquals(1, con.No_of_Open_Tasks__c, 'Incorrect number of open
tasks set on contact');
```

```
    //Now update the task status and commit the change

t.Status = 'Completed';

    update t;


    con = [SELECT No_of_Open_Tasks__c FROM Contact WHERE Id = :con.Id];
System.assertEquals(0, con.No_of_Open_Tasks__c, 'Incorrect number of open
tasks set on contact');

    }

}
```

As we can see, we now have to retrieve our contact record from the database using
the line:

```
Contact con = [SELECT Id FROM Contact LIMIT 1];
```

We know as we are in a test that there is only a single record in the database we can
see and that is the contact record the setupData method has created.

We could extend this out further to extract the contact creation into a test data factory
class which can be utilized by the @TestSetup annotated methods for all of our test
classes, however that is out of scope for our book, but you are encouraged to find out
more about this using the various open-source examples available online.

# Test.startTest and Test.stopTest

The final testing topic we will cover is that of working with Test.startTest and
Test.stopTest. Within our tests, we have performed a number of queries, DML
statements, and other statements which are all contributing towards the usage of our
governor limits. As our system grows and as we begin to construct more complex
tests, we may reach the point where our setup code prior to the code we are testing is
consuming a great enough proportion of the governor limits that it causes the test to
fail from a LimitException. This type of exception is thrown when a governor limit
is breached and is something we wish to avoid to ensure our code is scalable as we
grow in usage and volume over time.

Salesforce provides the Test.startTest and Test.stopTest methods to enable us to
execute a portion of the code within its own execution context and with its own set

of governor limits. We can call these methods once per test and the code in between these methods has a distinct set of governor limits to work with, to ensure that we can test our code for scalability appropriately.

To ensure that our trigger code was operating in its execution context and not exceeding governor limits or impacted by the test data creation, we could update our test class as follows:

```
@isTest

private with sharing class TaskTriggerHandler_Test {


    @TestSetup

    private static void setupData() {

        Contact con = new Contact();

con.FirstName = 'Marco';

con.LastName = 'Polo';

con.Phone = '111111111';

        insert con;

    }


@isTest

private static void testIncrementOnNewTask() {


//Create our test data

Contact con = [SELECT Id FROM Contact LIMIT 1];


Task t = new Task();

t.WhoId = con.Id;

t.Subject = 'Test task';
```

```
//Execute the code we want to test

Test.startTest();

insert t;

Test.stopTest();


//We need to retrieve the Contact record again to check the value has
been updated

con = [SELECT No_of_Open_Tasks__c FROM Contact WHERE Id = :con.Id];

System.assertEquals(1, con.No_of_Open_Tasks__c, 'Incoprrect number of
open tasks set on contact');

}


    @isTest
    private static void testDecrementOnClosedTask() {


        //Create our test data
        Contact con = [SELECT Id FROM Contact LIMIT 1];


        Task t = new Task();
t.WhoId = con.Id;
t.Subject = 'Test task';
        insert t;


        //Let us verify our data is setup correctly
        con = [SELECT No_of_Open_Tasks__c FROM Contact WHERE Id = :con.Id];
System.assertEquals(1, con.No_of_Open_Tasks__c, 'Incorrect number of open
tasks set on contact');
```

```
    //Now update the task status and commit the change

t.Status = 'Completed';

Test.startTest();

    update t;

Test.stopTest();


//Retrieve the Contact record again to check the value has been updated

        con = [SELECT No_of_Open_Tasks__c FROM Contact WHERE Id = :con.Id];

System.assertEquals(0, con.No_of_Open_Tasks__c, 'Incorrect number of open
tasks set on contact');

    }

}
```

Making this update would ensure that each of the DML statements we are testing run in their execution context and are not impacted by resource usage from the data setup code or assertion code. In the example shown above, this is not required, but when working with larger codebases and performing tests on volumes of records they should be used to avoid false failures.

# Conclusion

In this chapter, we have covered the fundamentals of testing on the Salesforce platform. Testing is a large topic and there are many other practices and features of the Apex testing framework we have not seen here, however, the information covered within this chapter should cover the majority of use cases and help you get started in testing your code[3]. Testing is one of the most important pieces of the development process and is often not given the due care and attention it deserves. I highly recommend as a best practice you ensure that you are always testing positive, negative, and bulk cases within your code, and for trigger code to test when working with over 200 records. Doing so will provide you with the greatest level of confidence that the code is performing as anticipated and can help ensure it is easier to maintain and manage in the future.

3   If you wish to undergo a broader deep dive into Apex testing, I have a 2 hour intensive course on testing available at https://bit.ly/astroApex.

Finally, I would also recommend that should a user, customer, or tester ever raise a bug with you around a piece of code that your first step be to replicate that bug within a unit test. This has a number of benefits:

- Provides a repeatable way of replicating the issue
- Provides a simple way of validating the issue has been fixed
- Improves the overall codebase for the future by adding additional testing around use cases that may not be considered during future updates.

# Questions

1. What code coverage percentage must be achieved in order to deploy Apex code to a production environment?
2. What is the annotation to mark a class as a test class?
3. What are the three steps of any test?
4. How can we test for exceptions?
5. What does a method annotate with `@TestSetup` do?
6. What do `System.startTest` and `System.stopTest` do?

# CHAPTER 12
# Callouts in Apex

One of the most common use cases developers will come across on Salesforce is the need to integrate with other external systems to either send or retrieve some data. In this chapter, we are going to look at this specific use case and how we can write Apex code to allow us to call APIs from other solutions.

## Structure

In this chapter we are going to learn:

- How we can integrate Salesforce with external systems using Apex
- How to add Remote Site Settings to enable callouts
- How to make HTTP requests in Apex with headers and body data
- How to handle HTTP responses
- How to test web service callouts in Apex

## Overview

By the end of this chapter you will know:

- How to make a REST request in Apex
- How to add body data and headers to an HTTP request

- How to serialize and deserialize JSON data
- How to test web service code

# REST vs. SOAP

Within the world of integrations, there are two main types of API, RESTful APIs, and SOAP-based APIs. **SOAP** stands for Simple Object Access Protocol and was the mainstay of integrations between systems for a number of years. When working with a SOAP-based API we have access to a web services description file (commonly referred to as a WSDL – pronounced "wuzdell" - as this is the extension of the file). This is an XML based file detailing the structure of the integration and available methods to call. For a strongly typed language like Apex, this allows tools that can take the definition file and construct classes for you to work with that make integration easier. One of the downsides however is that SOAP-based APIs communicate using XML which may include more descriptive information about the request and response. This can lead to large messages being sent back and forth in the API calls.

REST was designed as a way of allowing connected systems to communicate using the prebuilt standards of the web rather than a fixed protocol. **REST** standards for REpresentational State Transfer and uses the existing HTTP based communication protocols of the web to transfer data and represent the state. Unlike SOAP, REST has no typing and so can send data in a number of formats, including JSON (JavaScript Object Notation), which is much smaller and more appropriate for web and mobile-based applications.

Both SOAP and REST-based APIs have a variety of use cases, however, in this chapter, we are going to focus on working with RESTful APIs. This is because Salesforce provides a pre-built tool to take an existing WSDL file for a SOAP API and create a set of Apex classes to implement these methods. RESTful APIs on the other hand typically require a greater amount of code from scratch to implement and are the more commonly integrated with on the modern web.

# A brief overview of REST

Before we dive into writing some Apex to connect to a RESTful API, it is worth briefly covering how a RESTful API works. REST utilizes the standard HTTP protocol and URI schema used across the web to define APIs in a common format. A REST API transaction involves a request to the API and a response from the API. When we integrate with an API from Apex we will be writing the request and handling the response.

A request is composed of 4 items:

1.  An endpoint, that is the URI we are accessing
2.  A method, one of the standard HTTP methods, GET, POST, PUT, PATCH, or DELETE
3.  A header which may have a number of parameters in key-value pairs
4.  A body which contains additional details for our request

We will then receive a response to our request which will typically contain:

1.  A header which may have a number of parameters in key-value pairs
2.  A status code that indicates the success of the request
3.  A body which may contain data that we were requesting

We are going to be working with an API I have defined on Heroku for us to use for this book. This API will allow you to send me a message about what you thought of this book and see the messages others have left. Hopefully, as you have reached this point it will be a positive message, but I welcome all feedback on the book.

# Calling our webservice

If you visit www.learnsfdevwithapex.com you will see a list of messages that readers of this book such as yourself have sent me about the book as part of this chapter. This website has an API backend that we are going to develop an integration with. The website and the API are hosted on Heroku and are something I have custom developed for this book so that we have an API we can test against that is not going to change or require a lot of setups to work with.

Our API has 2 endpoints we can use, it has an endpoint that allows us to get a list of messages that have been submitted and are shown on the website and another endpoint that allows you to submit a message. Let us first deal with the retrieval of messages.

The API endpoint to retrieve messages is defined as follows:

**Endpoint**: /messages

**Method**: GET

**Returns**: A JSON object containing a `message` property that holds an array of messages. An example response body is:

```
[
{
id: "1",
```

```
body: "Test Message",

posted: "2020-04-18",

sender: "John Smith",

location: "Bury, UK"

}

]
```

Let us start by defining a new class called `LearningSFDevAPI`. We want our class to have a static method to retrieve the messages which for now we will have return void:

```
public class LearningSFDevAPI {

public static void getMessages() {

}

}
```

We need to use the Salesforce system class `HttpRequest` to build out our request to send. This is a system utility class that Salesforce has provided to make it easy for us to work with REST web services and manage the lifecycle of a request and a response. We begin by instantiating a new instance of the `HttpRequest` class:

```
public class LearningSFDevAPI {

public static void getMessages() {

HttpRequest req = new HttpRequest();

}

}
```

For this call we need to set both the endpoint for the request and the method:

```
public class LearningSFDevAPI {

public static void getMessages() {

HttpRequest req = new HttpRequest();

req.setMethod('GET');
```

```
req.setEndpoint('https://api.learnsfdevwithapex.com/messages');

}

}
```

This has defined a new HTTP request for us which we can use to retrieve the messages from our endpoint which is available at https://api.learnsfdevwithapex. com/messages. This is the simplest type of request that we can send, the API does not require any authentication, we have no headers, body, or parameters to set and thus we can simply make our request. In order to send the request and retrieve a response we have to use the Http class to send the request which will return a HttpResponse instance:

```
public class LearningSFDevAPI                                              {


public static void getMessages() {

HttpRequest req = new HttpRequest();

req.setMethod('GET');

req.setEndpoint('https://api.learnsfdevwithapex.com/messages');


Http http = new Http();

HttpResponse res = http.send(req);

System.debug(res.getBody());

                                                                          }



}
```

This will now send our request and output the body of the response to the debug logs. Before we can test this though, we need to add the domain to the allowed endpoints through **Remote Site Settings** in the **Setup** menu. Search for **remote** in the setup search bar and select **Remote Site Settings** from the filtered options. Create a new record with the details shown in *Figure 12.2* below and save:

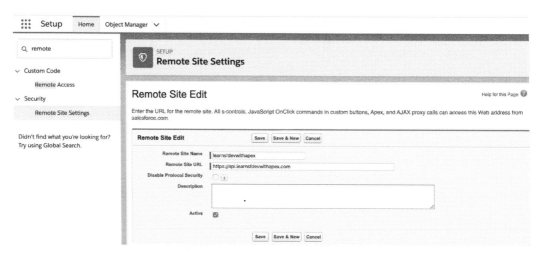

*Figure 12.1: Addition of the required remote site setting to allow our request to be made.*

Once you have done this and saved the `LearningSFDevAPI` class, you can run the following code in your Execute Anonymous window and view the debug logs to see the messages being returned.

```
LearningSFDevAPI.getMessages();
```

A set of records similar to our example body from the API definition should be printed to our logs. The body we are receiving back from the API is in **JSON (JavaScript Object Notation)** which whilst very lightweight and useful for sending data back and forth, is not something that our Apex code can work with natively. We have 2 options here, either we can parse the body and retrieve only certain data elements we need, navigating through the JSON object like a tree, or we can deserialize the JSON into an Apex data type. When we say *deserialize* we mean to parse the data from JSON into an Apex data type for manipulation

Because we know both the format of the data type and wish to be able to work with all the elements, we are going to deserialize to an Apex data type. There is no inbuilt Apex data type that will work for our message, so we must create one. This is the exact use case for an inner class which we discussed in *Chapter 9: Apex Classes*.

# Defining our inner class

From *Chapter 9: Apex Classes* we will recall that we define an inner class by simply declaring the class inside another class. In this instance, we are going to define a new inner class called `Message` which will hold one of our messages. For each of the attributes on the message we are receiving in the JSON response, we should add an attribute onto our class with the same name and the corresponding Apex data type. Our `Message` class would, therefore, be defined as follows within our `LearningSFDevAPI` class:

```
public class Message {

    public String id;

    public String body;

    public Date posted;

    public String sender;

    public String location;

}
```

This is a very simple class and simply allows us to create an Apex representation of the data we have received in a JSON format.

The next step is to deserialize the response from JSON into this Apex data type, or more accurately, a `List<Message>`. Why this data type? If you inspect the response body we are returned you will see that we are returning an array of data (the square brackets indicate an array in JSON) and so we are needing to create a list of items for our data. We deserialize using the `JSON.deserialize` method passing in 2 parameters, the JSON we wish to deserialize and the type we wish to deserialize to. Finally, I have updated the method to return the messages from our method so we can use them elsewhere in the system:

```
public class LearningSFDevAPI {


public static List<Message> getMessages() {

HttpRequest req = new HttpRequest();

req.setMethod('GET');

req.setEndpoint('https://api.learnsfdevwithapex.com/messages');


Http http = new Http();

HttpResponse res = http.send(req);

List<Message> messages = (List<Message>)(JSON.deserialize(res.getBody(),
List<Message>.class));
```

```
return messages;

}


public class Message {

    public String id;

    public String body;

    public Date posted;

    public String sender;

        public String location;

}

}
```

In the following line:

```
List<Message> messages = (List<Message>)(JSON.deserialize(res.getBody(),
List<Message>.class));
```

We are doing a set of steps that we should talk through.

`List<Message>` messages just defines a variable called messages with the type `List<Message>`. Moving to `JSON.deserialize(res.getBody(), List<Message>.class)`, the first parameter to `JSON.deserialize` is our JSON string from the response body, the second is the Apex data type we wish to cast to (you append `.class` to get the Apex data type definition). Finally, we have wrapped this within parentheses and then put the data type in parentheses before all this to cast the full result to the correct data type.

We could now use this new static method within our system to retrieve the messages and display them to an end-user or create Salesforce records from them if we want. Now we have looked at retrieving records, let us see how you can send a message for the site.

# Posting data to the site

We are now going to define a method that you can use to send a message to me which can feature on the site. Any messages that you send will be read by me and go through an approval just in case somebody decides to post anything that contains (for example) profanity. However, I am interested in all feedback and promise I will read every message.

In order to send a message we have to use the following endpoint:

**Endpoint**: /messages

**Method**: POST

**Body**: A valid message including the following attributes:

- body (String): The message to send
- email (String): A valid email address from you so that I can send you a personal thank you for your message
- sender (String): Your name to display on the site
- location (String): Where in the world you are from
- test (Boolean): Whether to commit the message (i.e. send it to me and the site) or just to test

**Headers**: The following header is required

- X-Auth-Token: An authentication token so that the site cannot be spammed

**Returns**: Either a success code or the relevant error

We should define a new method called sendMessage in our class which takes in a Message object instance for us to post. To do this we will also need to update our Message class to add in some additional parameters. Let us first do this:

```
public class LearningSFDevAPI                                    {


public static List<Message> getMessages() {

HttpRequest req = new HttpRequest();

req.setMethod('GET');

req.setEndpoint('https://api.learnsfdevwithapex.com/messages');


Http http = new Http();

HttpResponse res = http.send(req);

List<Message> messages = (List<Message>)(JSON.deserialize(res.getBody(),
List<Message>.class));
```

```
return messages;

}


public class Message {

    public String id;

    public String body;

    public Date posted;

    public String sender;

        public String location;

public String email;

public Boolean test;

}

}
```

These additional variables will allow us to serialize our `Message` instance to send it as part of our request. We now need to define our `sendMessage` method which takes in the `Message` instance and constructs our request. Firstly the method definition:

```
public static void sendMessage(Message msg) {


}
```

We then need to construct an `HttpRequest` instance again, using the same endpoint but the `POST` method:

```
public static void sendMessage(Message msg) {

HttpRequest req = new HttpRequest();

req.setMethod('POST');

req.setEndpoint('https://api.learnsfdevwithapex.com/messages');

}
```

We then want to set the body for our request to be the serialized version of the `Message` instance we have been passed:

```
public static void sendMessage(Message msg) {

HttpRequest req = new HttpRequest();

req.setMethod('POST');

req.setEndpoint('https://api.learnsfdevwithapex.com/messages');

req.setBody(JSON.serialize(msg));

}
```

The API also requires us to set the X-Auth-Token header. This is a value that will allow the system to check that you have read this book before calling the API. The token we will use to authenticate will simply be the string LearningSFDevAPI. To set this we use the setHeader method on our request, passing in X-Auth-Token as the first parameter (the key) and our token as the value:

```
public static void sendMessage(Message msg) {

HttpRequest req = new HttpRequest();

req.setMethod('POST');

req.setEndpoint('https://api.learnsfdevwithapex.com/messages');

req.setBody(JSON.serialize(msg));

req.setHeader('X-Auth-Token', 'LearningSFDevAPI');

}
```

Finally, we need to send the request and will debug the response. Our final class looks like:

```
public class LearningSFDevAPI {


public static List<Message> getMessages() {

HttpRequest req = new HttpRequest();

req.setMethod('GET');

req.setEndpoint('https://api.learnsfdevwithapex.com/messages');


Http http = new Http();
```

```
HttpResponse res = http.send(req);

List<Message> messages = (List<Message>)(JSON.deserialize(res.getBody(),
List<Message>.class));

return messages;

}


public static void sendMessage(Message msg) {

HttpRequest req = new HttpRequest();

req.setMethod('POST');

req.setEndpoint('https://api.learnsfdevwithapex.com/messages');

req.setBody(JSON.serialize(msg));


Http http = new Http();

HttpResponse res = http.send(req);

System.debug(res);

    }


public class Message {

    public String id;

    public String body;

    public Date posted;

    public String sender;

        public String location;

public String email;

public Boolean test;

    }

    }
```

You can now test this using the following Execute Anonymous (you can set your own values for body, sender, email, and location):

```
LearningSFDevAPI.Message msg = new LearningSFDevAPI.Message();

msg.body = 'TEST MESSAGE';

msg.sender = 'Paul Battisson';

msg.email = 'paul@cloudbites.tv';

msg.location = 'Harrogate, UK';

msg.test = true;


LearningSFDevAPI.sendMessage(msg);
```

If you inspect the debug logs for our debug statement you should see:

```
DEBUG|System.HttpResponse\[Status=OK, StatusCode=200\]
```

When you are ready, feel free to change the test parameter from true to false and send me a message on your feedback for the book!

We have now seen how we can send a couple of different API requests both sending and receiving data. In our code so far though we have only handled the OK statuses. We should also add some logic in our response handlers to deal with other issues (i.e. exceptions). Typically, in the instance where the response is not an OK or 200 status code, we should throw an exception detailing the response from the API. We can do this by adding some logic to the response object we have in our methods.

Firstly we can define a new custom exception class:

```
public class LearningSFDevAPIException extends Exception   {


}
```

And then whenever we get a response that is not a 200/OK response throw that exception to stop our code executing. For example:

```
public class LearningSFDevAPI {

public static List<Message> getMessages() {

HttpRequest req = new HttpRequest();
```

```apex
req.setMethod('GET');

req.setEndpoint('https://api.learnsfdevwithapex.com/messages');


Http http = new Http();

HttpResponse res = http.send(req);

if(res.getStatusCode() == 200) {

List<Message> messages = (List<Message>)(JSON.deserialize(res.getBody(),
List<Message>.class));

return messages;

} else {

throw new LearningSFDevAPIException('API callout returned with a status
of ' + res.getStatus());

}

}


public static void sendMessage(Message msg) {

HttpRequest req = new HttpRequest();

req.setMethod('POST');

req.setEndpoint('https://api.learnsfdevwithapex.com/messages');

req.setBody(JSON.serialize(msg));


Http http = new Http();

HttpResponse res = http.send(req);

if(res.getStatusCode() != 200) {

throw new LearningSFDevAPIException('API callout returned with a status
of ' + res.getStatus());

}

}
```

```
public class Message {

    public String id;

    public String body;

    public Date posted;

    public String sender;

        public String location;

public String email;

public Boolean test;

}

}
```

In this updated code you can see in the getMessages method we are checking the response has the 200 status code and then deserializing our data, otherwise throwing an error. In the sendMessage method, we are instead checking for a status code that is not 200 and throwing the error as our default behavior is to just continue and not return any data.

When working with APIs you should make sure you understand how the business wishes to handle these exceptions and deal with them. In some cases, erring and stopping execution is correct. In some situations, you may want to retry or create a log record.

# Testing web services

Now we have our Apex code to call the web service, we need to write some test code to ensure this works as expected. In order to test the web service, we are going to use a mock class. Mocking is the process by which we provide a dummy implementation of some code to enable us to test the solution appropriately when either the full implementation is unavailable (as we have here - we cannot make callouts in tests), or when we want to test only the interface between classes and not the implementation itself. A discussion around dependency injection and mocking is outside the scope of this book but is something that the reader should investigate as they begin to write more complex applications on the platform.

There are 2 ways of mocking a web service callout in Apex, through a coded implementation of the HttpCallouMock class or the use of a static resource combined with the StaticResourceCalloutMock class. We will see both examples here.

# StaticResourceCalloutMock

The StaticResourceCalloutMock class allows a developer to provide a JSON body in a Static Resource along with a set of parameters that an Apex test will use in place of the actual callout. Create a JSON file (a file with the extension .json) in a text editor on your local machine that contains the following:

```
[

{

"id": "1",

"body": "Test Message",

"posted": "2020-04-18",

"sender": "John Smith",

"location": "Bury, UK"

}

]
```

This is our example response for the GET API endpoint and we will use this in testing. Upload this to Salesforce as a Static Resource (go to the **Setup** menu, search for **Static Resources**, and create a new resource as shown below, select your file for the input):

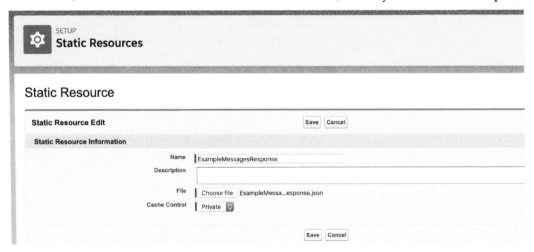

*Figure 12.2: Static Resource definition*

Now create a new Apex class for our test called LearningSFDevAPI_Test. In the class we want to define a method called testGetMessages as shown:

```
@isTest

private class LearningSFDevAPI_Test {


@isTest

private static void testGetMessages() {


}

}
```

Next for our test data setup, we are going to instantiate a new instance of StaticResourceCalloutMock, set the correct parameters and tell it to use our newly created static resource and inform our test framework to use it:

```
@isTest

private class LearningSFDevAPI_Test          {


@isTest

private static void testGetMessages()   {


StaticResourceCalloutMock mock = new StaticResourceCalloutMock();

mock.setStaticResource('ExampleMessagesResponse');

mock.setStatusCode(200);

mock.setHeader('Content-Type', 'application/json');


Test.setMock(HttpCalloutMock.class, mock);


}

}
```

The first 4 lines of our test are setting up the StaticResourceCalloutMock instance to use our resource and also return the correct status. The Test.setMock method tells the Apex test runner to return the static resource contents as the body from the callout, with the headers and status code we define. We can then test the calling of the method and assert that we receive one message back:

```
@isTest
private class LearningSFDevAPI_Test          {


@isTest
private static void testGetMessages()        {


StaticResourceCalloutMock mock = new StaticResourceCalloutMock();
mock.setStaticResource('ExampleMessagesResponse');
mock.setStatusCode(200);
mock.setHeader('Content-Type', 'application/json');


Test.setMock(HttpCalloutMock.class, mock);


List<LearningSFDevAPI.Message> messages = LearningSFDevAPI.getMessages();
System.assertEquals(1, messages.size(), 'Incorrect number of messages returned');


}
}
```

If we save this and run the test it will pass and reviewing the code coverage on the LearningSFDevAPI class will show it is executing our code as we expect.

# Custom HttpCalloutMock implementation

The alternative option we have for testing is to use a custom implementation of the HttpCalloutMock interface. We have seen in *Chapter 10: Apex Class Inheritance* how we can implement an interface, and the HttpCalloutMock interface is implemented by `StaticResourceCalloutMock` to provide the functionality we have just seen. Custom implementation can be useful for more prescriptive testing examples or where a response body may vary over time or be more dynamic. We are going to test the remainder of our `getMessages` method using a custom `HttpCalloutMock` implementation. Firstly, we should define a new class called `LearningSFDevAPIMock` and mark it to implement the `HttpCalloutMock` interface:

```
public class LearningSFDevAPIMock implements HttpCalloutMock {


}
```

This interface has a single method to implement, `respond`. This method takes in an `HttpRequest` object instance and returns a `HttpResponse` instance we will generate. We want our response to return a 418 status code which signifies `I'm a Teapot`. This status code is a valid error status and is a joke that was introduced into the HTTP specification in 1998 as an April Fool's Prank. It has however remained in use and will serve us here as an error status to work with. Let us implement the `respond` method and return the status `I'm a little teapot` with a status code of 418:

```
public class LearningSFDevAPIMock implements HttpCalloutMock {

public HTTPResponse respond(HTTPRequest req) {

HttpResponse res = new HTTPResponse();

res.setStatusCode(418);

res.setStatus('I\'m a teapot');

        return res;

    }

}
```

We can then define our next test method `testGetMessagesException` as:

```
@isTest

private static void testGetMessagesException()         {


LearningSFDevAPIMock mock = new LearningSFDevAPIMock();
```

```
Test.setMock(HttpCalloutMock.class, mock);


try {

List<LearningSFDevAPI.Message> messages = LearningSFDevAPI.getMessages();

System.assert(false);

} catch(LearningSFDevAPIException ex) {

System.assert(ex.getMessage().contains('I\'m a teapot'), ex.getMessage());

                                                                             }


}
```

You can see in this test we have also used our exception catching pattern for tests we discussed in the last chapter. Saving these updated classes and running our tests again, our getMessages method is now completely covered. It is left as an exercise for the reader to test the sendMessage method.

# Security and authentication

In the examples we have been working within this chapter we have had very basic or no authentication for the API to concern ourselves with. This has been done purposefully to allow us to focus on the task of writing the Apex code and explaining the detail in the steps to define a callout. However, in most circumstances, an API will require you to authenticate using a mechanism such as OAuth. Whilst you can write a custom handler for this in Apex, it is more expedient to use a feature called Named Credentials to manage this for you.

Named Credentials allow you to define an endpoint and authentication mechanism for an API that can be used across your code and avoid the need to have the endpoint URL defined in multiple locations. A full discussion of setting up Named Credentials for the many different authentication mechanisms is out of scope, however, we can define a Named Credential, as shown in *Figure 12.4*, for our API that we can use.

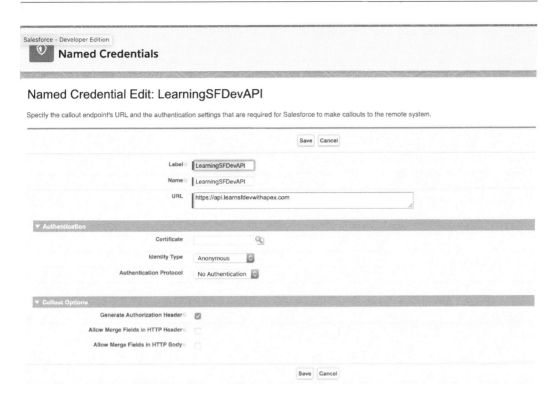

*Figure 12.3: Named Credential definition*

We can then update our existing class code to utilize this:

```
public class LearningSFDevAPI {


public static List<Message> getMessages() {

HttpRequest req = new HttpRequest();

req.setMethod('GET');

req.setEndpoint('callout:LearningSFDevAPI/messages');


Http http = new Http();

HttpResponse res = http.send(req);

if(res.getStatusCode() == 200) {

List<Message> messages = (List<Message>)(JSON.deserialize(res.getBody(),
```

```
List<Message>.class));

return messages;

} else {

throw new LearningSFDevAPIException('API callout returned with a status
of ' + res.getStatus());

}

}


public static void sendMessage(Message msg) {

HttpRequest req = new HttpRequest();

req.setMethod('POST');

req.setEndpoint('callout:LearningSFDevAPI/messages');

req.setBody(JSON.serialize(msg));


Http http = new Http();

HttpResponse res = http.send(req);

if(res.getStatusCode() != 200) {

throw new LearningSFDevAPIException('API callout returned with a status
of ' + res.getStatus());

}

}


public class Message {

    public String id;

    public String body;

    public Date posted;

    public String sender;
```

```
        public String location;

public String email;

public Boolean test;

}

}
```

Now if the URL for the API were to change, we could simply update the Named Credential and this would all still work. Again, with stronger authentication methods, the use of Named Credentials also allows developers to abstract away the authentication logic from the rest of the API code to improve manageability and maintainability.

# Conclusion

In this chapter, we have learned how to integrate our system with a custom endpoint using Apex. We have seen how to define requests and handle responses from endpoints, including sending and receiving data. We also looked at how we can test endpoints using the `HttpCalloutMock` interface and `StaticResourceCalloutMock` to enable us to test our callout and parsing code works as anticipated.

As a developer, you will often be asked to integrate with a third-party solution. Before writing any code, you should spend time to ensure that you have verified there is no standard connector or library available. This can save you a lot of time in the long run. You should try to layer your API application code, too many developers start by trying to build an all-encompassing library for the third party endpoints when they will only be using a couple of requests. Finally, we saw how to use Named Credentials to improve the security and maintainability of our API code. Wherever possible you should use Named Credentials to ensure that you have a single place for the definition of an API endpoint and its security needs. This has the added benefit of allowing the endpoint's URL and information to be manageable by an administrator in the future should it change.

# Questions

1. What are the different methods available for a HTTP Request?
2. What are the 3 ways we have seen for testing web service callouts?
3. What is the difference between REST and SOAP?
4. Why should we use a Named Credential?

# CHAPTER 13
# Conclusion

When I began planning this book I wanted to provide a way for a broad range of people to learn Apex in a manner that made most sense to me. In the time I have been working with Salesforce, I have been lucky enough to have worked with some very smart people who have helped me to make sense of it all and understand the nuances of the platform. I have also taught many people how to learn Apex, both in my day job and as a Salesforce Certified Instructor. Doing so has helped me to understand where some of the more difficult roadblocks are and where people most often struggle, which hopefully I have eased with this book.

Salesforce is a very unique ecosystem in that large volumes of those delivering solutions are not from a stereotypical computer science background, myself included. I taught myself how to program computers as a bored teenager who was into science and maths and wanted to make his own games. For those trying to learn Apex who do not have an extensive professional programming background, be they a graduate coming out of university or a Salesforce administrator/functional consultant, it can feel like an uphill struggle where many of the signposts on the road are missing.

Salesforce provide a plethora of free tools to help individuals to learn to code, including the developer documentation and Trailhead modules.

There is no shortage of materials available on YouTube or in blogs. The aim for this book was to allow you to have some written material that aims to explain why things are done in a certain way and layer the knowledge of the language for you. Hopefully it meets that aim.

So, what next now you have finished the book? My first bit of advice is to start building. If you are in work where use cases are readily available, take the opportunity to try and implement (or reimplement) some use cases yourself. Then, most importantly, spend time reviewing the solutions you have built and think about how you can improve them.

Sadly, most people do not treat learning a new programming language in the same way they treat learning a new spoken language. When attempting to learn Spanish for example, you would daily try to write some Spanish, speak some Spanish, and read some Spanish to help cement the concepts. I encourage you to try the same for your learning of Apex. Try and write some Apex code everyday to ensure you are understanding how to create and deploy Apex. Talk with colleagues about the work you and they are doing to try and speak about Apex. That might be anything from "Hey Laura, can I talk to you about that code you are writing?" to attending a local TrailBlazer Community Developer Group. And read Apex. The Salesforce ecosystem is full of people who have shared millions of lines of Apex code for you to review and try to understand, and more importantly, think "what would I do differently?" No code is perfect.

There are also many videos and courses out there to build on this book and help you to understand certain topics more deeply. This book should only be seen as the beginning on your journey into the world of programming on the Salesforce platform.

Finally, I sincerely want to thank you for reading this book and hope you have found it useful. Please do complete the exercise in *Chapter 12: Callouts in Apex* and let me know your thoughts. You can also find me on Twitter as @pbattisson should you wish to hear more from me about Salesforce and other things tech related.

Thank you, and happy coding.

Printed in Great Britain
by Amazon